Also by Sebastian Junger

Tribe

War

A Death in Belmont

Fire

The Perfect Storm

FREEDOM

Sebastian Junger

Simon & Schuster

NEW YORK · LONDON · TORONTO
SYDNEY · NEW DELHI

Simon & Schuster
1230 Avenue of the Americas
New York, NY 10020

Copyright © 2021 by Sebastian Junger

First Simon & Schuster hardcover edition May 2021

SIMON & SCHUSTER and colophon are registered trademarks
of Simon & Schuster, Inc.

For information about special discounts for bulk purchases,
please contact Simon & Schuster Special Sales at 1-866-506-1949
or business@simonandschuster.com.

The Simon & Schuster Speakers Bureau can bring authors to your
live event. For more information or to book an event, contact the
Simon & Schuster Speakers Bureau at 1-866-248-3049
or visit our website at www.simonspeakers.com.

Interior design by Paul Dippolito

Manufactured in the United States of America

1   3   5   7   9   10   8   6   4   2

Library of Congress Cataloging-in-Publication Data
Names: Junger, Sebastian, author.
Title: Freedom / By Sebastian Junger.
Description: First Simon & Schuster hardcover edition. | New York, NY :
Simon & Schuster, [2021] | Includes bibliographical references. |
Summary: "A profound rumination on the concept of freedom from the
New York Times bestselling author of Tribe"— Provided by publisher.
Identifiers: LCCN 2020056780 (print) | LCCN 2020056781 (ebook) | ISBN
9781982153410 (hardcover) | ISBN 9781982153427 (paperback) | ISBN
9781982153434 (ebook)
Subjects: LCSH: Liberty—United States—History. | Courage—United
States—History. | United States—Social life and customs.
Classification: LCC JC599.U62 J86 2021 (print) | LCC JC599.U62 (ebook) |
DDC 323.440973—dc23
LC record available at https://lccn.loc.gov/2020056780
LC ebook record available at https://lccn.loc.gov/2020056781
ISBN 978-1-9821-5341-0
ISBN 978-1-9821-5343-4 (ebook)

To my beloved family, who taught me
the true meaning of freedom

Contents

BOOK ONE · RUN

BOOK TWO · FIGHT

BOOK THREE · THINK

*As for humans, God tests them so they
may know they are animals.*

—Ecclesiastes 3:18 (NIV)

BOOK ONE · RUN

T he change was immediate. The country opened up west of Harrisburg and suddenly we could drink from streams and build fires without getting caught and sleep pretty much anywhere we wanted. We'd walked the railroad tracks from Washington to Baltimore to Philly and then turned west at the Main Line and made Amish country by winter. The Pennsylvania fields lay bare and hard in the cold but there were seams and folds in that country—strips of woods along stream bottoms, windbreaks between the cornfields, ridges left wild for hunting—where a man could easily pass the night unnoticed. Once, we cooked dinner on a steep hill above the town of Christiana and went to sleep in a snowstorm listening to the clatter of carriage horses on the street below. At dawn we walked into town for pancakes and coffee and then headed on up the railroad tracks before anyone whose job it was to stop us even knew we'd been there.

But outside Harrisburg, where the Juniata River runs into the Susquehanna at her great breaching of Blue Mountain, we seemed to have been simply released into the wild.

Early settlers tended to push up the major rivers until they ran into the first set of waterfalls—the "fall line"—and those spots became jumping-off points for people who were even more desperate or adventurous. At Blue Mountain the Susquehanna drops down a series of ledges and deepens in the alluvial soil of the coastal plain, and that was where a Welsh émigré named John Harris established a business poling rafts across the river in the 1730s. What was then called "Indian country" effectively started on the other side, and when Harris's passengers stepped ashore they found themselves in a forest of enormous hardwoods that extended almost unbroken for the next thousand miles, to the Great Plains.

They were trappers and traders and fugitives from justice and young men scouting land for their families and eventually the families themselves. Many came on heavy oak-frame wagons that were caulked like boats and carried everything—food, tools, crockery, fabric, maybe an heirloom quilt—that the forest couldn't provide. The wagons were low-slung for stability and tented with canvas and had iron-strapped wheels six inches wide that had no shock absorbers whatsoever. The men walked with long-barreled flintlock rifles over their shoulders and the women rode if they were pregnant and walked otherwise and the children were up and down off the wagons all day long. These people made their way up the western bank of the Susquehanna, through the Blue Mountain gap, and then turned onto the Juniata, which ran fast and clear all the way from the great escarpments of the Alleghenies. She was the only river valley that led west in the entire state and became a threshold of sorts—to a better life, or an early death—for thousands of settlers who headed into the wilderness without any intention of returning.

Three hundred years later we walked through a cluster of camper-trailers between the river and some standard-gauge railroad and then climbed onto the tracks themselves. We could hear trucks downshifting on the last hill before Harrisburg on Route 22, across the river. It was late April, and the Juniata was running fast and full in the spring flood, an occasional tree rolling in her current that had been undercut along the banks and toppled. She flowed between ridges that looked too steep to climb and ran compass-straight for miles. There were creeks for fresh water and floodwrack for firewood and woods so thick you could practically sleep within sight of a church steeple or police station and no one would know.

It struck us as serious country, the kind where you kept an eye on the weather and slept next to whatever weapon you had. All we had was a machete but after dark we all knew where it was—usually thunked into a tree somewhere central. Gunfire occasionally bounced off the shelf rock and detritus of the upper ridges and one morning an A-10 thundered through so low that we could almost make out the pilot in the cockpit. Not two days' walk from Harrisburg we passed a sign nailed to a tree that warned the federal government that the property "would be defended by any means necessary." There were meth addicts in some of the towns and black bears up on the ridges and the remains of old locks and canals along the river that almost looked ready to be returned to good use if history ever required it.

We walked single file on the cinder maintenance road that ran between the trackbed and the river. Creeks chased down off the ridges like they were fleeing something. Swarms of gnats worked the sunlight and bass boats spun past on the current below us. Where the tracks ran straight we saw trains from a mile or more, headlights boring toward us like fierce little suns, but even on the curves we often had a sense that a great force was headed our way. The trains were so heavy and fast that they seemed to set the whole world in motion, vibrating the air and raising a strange pitch from the rail that fell at the edge of human hearing. We got so attuned out there that we'd know a train was coming without even knowing *how* we knew—but we knew. We'd step into the underbrush and sit on our packs and some of us would roll a cigarette or drink water and we'd wait for the beast to come through. Freights moved at familiar speeds and took a full minute to go by, but the passenger trains could hit 140 and walloped past so suddenly, they just left us in a vortex of dead leaves and trash.

We took ten-minute breaks every hour and walked all afternoon. Occasionally in the distance we'd see a pickup truck nose out onto the tracks at an ungated farm road and then bounce across. Once we saw a car stopped in the middle of a bridge a mile or so ahead, and we put our binoculars on it to make sure it wasn't a cop. (It is illegal to trespass on railroad property, and on high-speed lines it is even considered a national security issue.) At the end of the day we came to an old quarrystone kiln at a place called Bailey Run, where a creek sawed through a ridge and ran under the tracks into the Juniata. The water was ice cold and filtered through the chert and limestone of the country and tasted as though civilization was still something in the future. We walked up the creek and made camp in a little stand of sycamore and hemlock that was nestled into the curve of a ridge. The only way to see our cookfire was to come down on us quietly through the woods at night, but we had a dog and that wasn't going to happen, either.

Juniata means "standing stone" in what used to be the Native languages of the area. Standing stones were granite or

7

sandstone pillars that were driven into the ground to mark the center of a tribe's territory. The earliest mention of the name appears on maps drawn by Dutch traders who visited Chesapeake Bay in the 1600s and wrote "Onojutta Haga" on the spot where the Juniata empties into the Susquehanna. Haga means "people" in Mohawk, and Onojutta means "protruding stone." Other recorded versions of the word include Chenegaide, Yuchniada, and Choniate; Europeans were at pains to write Native words because the languages sounded so alien.

The Onojutta-Haga are thought to be an offshoot of the Seneca, but they were wiped out early on, so no one knows for sure. There was another standing stone in northern New York and several natural ones in Ohio; they are rare things. One of the Onojutta-Haga villages was just a few miles from the confluence of the Frankstown Branch and the Little Juniata, which come together to form the Big Juniata at what is now the town of Huntingdon. It was a strategic spot: one well-used Indian trail led east-west along the Juniata from Chesapeake to Ohio, and another went north-south from New York to the Carolinas. The latter, known as the Warriors Path, was used by most of the local tribes when they raided traditional enemies hundreds of miles to the south.

At some point before Europeans arrived—probably long before—the Onojutta-Haga erected a fourteen-foot standing stone on that important crossroads. It was carved with signs and symbols of the tribe and possibly reflected a belief that their ancestors had emerged from the ground at that very spot. By the time the first Europeans got there, however, the Onojutta-Haga were gone, wiped out by the Iroquois conquests of the 1600s. Using guns supplied by Dutch fur traders, the five-nation Iroquois Confederacy effectively tried to take over everything east of the Mississippi and north of the Carolinas. They fought and eventually destroyed the Cat Nation of Ohio—also known as the Erie—leaving behind nothing "but great droves of wolves." They walked five hundred miles to destroy the Cherokee and Choctaw of Carolina. They sent a thousand men into Ontario to overrun the Huron. They forced the Shawnee and the Delaware and the Mingo into a kind of vassal servitude. And they easily dispatched the smaller tribes of eastern Pennsylvania: the Great Flats People, as the Iroquois called them, around the Wyoming Valley; the Cave Devils of the West Branch; and the Onojutta-Haga. All that remained was the name of the river, and their stone.

Settlers working their way up the Juniata in the early 1700s faced a wall of wilderness inhabited by some of the most warlike people on the planet. The Natives were better fed than the Europeans and tended to be taller and more muscular. Some dressed in the skins of bears and wolves and even wore the head over their own, as if they were that animal. Captain John Smith met a Susquehannock with a wolf's skull hung around his neck like a huge piece of jewelry. During combat they carried musket balls in their mouths for easy reloading and moved through the forest so quickly and quietly that colonial forces often thought they were fighting five or ten times as many warriors as they actually were.

By the early 1700s, the Iroquois had incorporated a sixth nation, the Tuscarora, into their confederacy and were at the height of their power. They declared the limit of colonial society to be the "Endless Mountains"—the easternmost ranges of the Alleghenies—that cut across northeastern Pennsylvania and continued to Tennessee. In many places the front range consisted of a single steep ridge, called Kittatinny by the Iroquois, that ran from New Paltz, New York, to the outskirts of Knoxville. It is so unwaveringly straight that on a map it almost looks drawn by a ruler. Too steep to easily climb and too long to go around, Kittatinny had only a handful of passages in her entire 250-mile length, including the great breach at Harrisburg. A few miles upstream, the Juniata comes bolting out of the last of her valleys and gorges.

Not only did Native autonomy begin at the mouth of the Juniata, but in a sense white autonomy did as well. The colonial government had little authority beyond that point and even less means to impose it. If you were willing to risk being captured by Indians and skinned alive or carved into pieces so that you could watch yourself be fed to dogs, then you could make your way up the finger valleys of the Juniata and find a secluded spot to build a cabin and get in a quick crop of corn. There was nothing there but you, the land, and God, and if you were still alive after the harvest, you could send for your family and make a go of it. Maybe you could convince some other families to come with you. The risks were appalling and the hardships unspeakable, but no government official would ever again tell you what to do.

Outside of actual wilderness, the narrow swaths of property that run alongside railroad lines are probably the least monitored in the country. If you had to cross a chunk of America without anyone knowing—if you were a fugitive, say, or broke and worried about vagrancy charges, or just didn't want to talk to anyone—you'd do well to choose the kind of railroad lines that run up the Juniata. There are almost no police on railroad lines, no suspicious homeowners, no dogs, no security cameras, and no floodlights. And geographically, railroad lines are pathologically efficient. They transect swamps, split towns, bore holes through mountains, and run secant across graceful riverbends. Railroad lines will never make you waste a step or walk up a hill, and if you're walking all day long, that's pretty much all you want out of a route.

The rails are high-quality steel rolled at the foundry into thirty-nine-foot lengths that weigh around one ton and are welded into sections almost a quarter mile long. The continuous-welded rail, as it's called, is laid onto steel tie plates spiked into wood crossties that sit on beds of crushed rock called top ballast. The top ballast is irregular and hard to walk on and the ties are spaced twenty-one inches apart which, coincidentally or not, falls midway between a long stride and short stride. It is extraordinarily hard to walk on railroad track.

Track is often laid in summer so that in winter it contracts with cold into a state of tension. Straight sections are called tangents and designed to absorb the sudden load of a mile-long, thirty-million-pound freight train moving sixty miles an hour. On curves the tracks are banked—also known as super-elevation—so that the load remains the same despite the centrifugal force, but if a train goes too slowly, it will sit heavily on the inner rail and wear it down. Railroad steel will also creep lengthwise or buckle sideways despite stabilizing anchors, and "pumper" ties will collect rainwater beneath them and shoot it sideways when trains pass over. The brakes on freight trains get very hot, and when pumper ties spray cold water on them, the brakes can crack and derail the train. Every component of a railroad track will eventually loosen, warp, break, or fail, which means that railroad lines are constantly being worked on by repair crews. Much of the 140,000 miles of railroad line in America has no original components left at all.

Because of the constant need for repairs, many of the railroad lines in America have packed-cinder maintenance roads running alongside them. That was the easiest walking to be had out there; it didn't kick out from under your back foot like top ballast and was so even that you could keep your eyes downtrack while you walked. You could even walk at night without a headlamp. On packed cinder there's a cadence that carries you three miles an hour fairly easily and another at four miles an hour that feels almost twice the effort. (The ancient Celtic measurement of a "league" was defined as the distance a man could walk in an hour—roughly three or four miles.) A heavy pack can give you a feeling of momentum that almost feels easier than walking with nothing at all, but a sixty-pound pack probably cuts your capability in half. And on a hot day the extra weight generates so much friction in your shoes that you can destroy the bottoms of your feet in hours. Once, I got such bad blisters that I took a curved sailmaker's needle and ran thread through them so they would drain at night. They got infected anyway and I couldn't walk right for a week.

The first hour is usually the hardest because you're not in cadence yet and every step requires its own little decision. Cadence sometimes descends on the entire group at once and can produce a strange feeling of elation. You know you're in cadence when walking feels easier than *not* walking. You know you're in cadence when you stop talking or even thinking and just walk. You'll know you're in cadence when the rhythm of everyone's footsteps coalesces into a long complex tattoo that evolves over hours and bears you along like the current of an invisible river you've been seeking your whole life.

Cadence can only carry you for so long before your body starts to fail, but even that's not the end. Sometimes you enter a great blank place where a whole hour can seem to go by faster than some of the minutes within it, and the loyal dog of your body trots along as if the entire point of its existence is to expire following your orders. It's a kind of fugue state that is weirdly easier to resist than the thin weakness that can creep up unexpectedly and petition you all morning long with its cheap little deals: take a break now and walk more later. Back off the pace and walk a little longer. Unless you confront this little traitor head-on it's only a matter of time before you will start to listen. Drop a discarded steel tie plate into your pack for a few miles or take the pace up a notch. Once I felt so weak that the only thing I could think to do was start running.

The poor have always walked and the desperate have always slept outside. We were neither, but we were still doing something that felt ancient and hard. Most Americans did not own a car until after World War Two, and "traveling" often meant walking out your front door and not stopping. During the Great Depression, one-quarter of the labor force had no work and there were so many Americans on the move that rural schoolhouses were often left unlocked so travelers could find shelter for the night. Schools always had a well to draw water for the horses and benches for the children to sleep on. Families generally stayed in the schoolhouses and lone men slept in people's barns—when they were lucky—or simply out in the woods.

We walked around four hundred miles and most nights we were the only people in the world who knew where we were. There are many definitions of *freedom* but surely that is one of them. We slept under bridges and in abandoned buildings and in the woods and on golf courses and once on a strip of sand on the western shore of Chesapeake Bay. The poor neighborhoods were easy to walk through because people would offer us water or ask if we were okay; in affluent areas they were more likely to call the cops. Walking through a rough stretch into Wilmington one night a car pulled up and a young black man stuck his head out of the passenger window. "Hey, where you all headed?" he asked. I told him up the East Coast and then to Pittsburgh. "You can come with us if you want," I said. Without a word he started to open the car door until a female hand grabbed his arm and pulled him back in. "Oh, no you don't," she said, and the car went fishtailing off down the street.

Whoever he was he wasn't *really* going to join us—it was a joke—the funny part presumably being that even walking to Pittsburgh with four men he didn't know was more appealing than staying home. And then there was the old man, a white guy, we met one freezing winter morning west of Lancaster, Pennsylvania. His car was parked along the tracks and we sat behind a sand berm studying him with binoculars for half an hour before deciding he wasn't a cop. When we walked up, he said, "I'll be back in half an hour with my gear if you'll let me come." I shook my head—whatever he was trying to get away from, I didn't want to be his ticket—but he still gave us his phone number. "Call if you change your mind," he said. "The cold weather doesn't bother me at all."

He wasn't joking and he didn't ask where we were going; he just wanted in. Or out. You had to wonder about a man who saw four men walking along railroad tracks in midwinter and thought they had more to offer than his life at that moment. He didn't need us in order to walk out his own front door, but lots of things that look like freedom when you're with other people are just a form of exile when you're alone, and vagrancy might be one of them. But the inside joke about freedom—he would have found out soon enough—is that you're always trading obedience to one thing for obedience to another. Whatever the man was fleeing, it couldn't have been more onerous than living outside in the middle of winter, but he clearly didn't care. The tasks we gave each other were minor—collect firewood, scrub the cookpots—but they were crucial to our existence and utterly nonnegotiable. Doing them meant you were one of us. Not doing them meant you were on your own. The choice was yours.

North of Wilmington we saw five or six guys sitting on lawn chairs next to a row of motorcycles in the parking lot of a low cement building. It was an empty, ruined-looking part of town that already had us on edge, but we asked if we could fill our water bottles because we were completely empty. The men were friendly in that kind of intense, aggressive way that can flip straight into violence, and I didn't want to be there long enough for that to happen. I collected our water bottles and went inside to fill them, and when my eyes adjusted to the darkness, I saw two huge men sitting shoulder to shoulder behind a plank desk. "Bullshit," one of them said when he saw me. "Bullshit bullshit bullshit."

They turned out to be "one-percenters"—criminals—who belonged to one of the first black motorcycle gangs in the country. They protected each other from rivals in exchange for absolute loyalty—the oldest deal in the world. "We can go anywhere we want in the entire country," one of them said. "The police just stay out of our way."

The freedom that comes from being feared is tempting for people who have suffered that fear themselves, as many one-percenters probably have. For people raised in safety, freedom can seem like a luxury, like money or good health, but first and foremost, it's the absence of threat. A person who can be killed without any consequences for the killers is not free in the most important sense of the word, and imagining otherwise probably means that the systems that keep you safe in your life—the armies, the police officers, the laws—are so unobtrusive, you've simply stopped noticing them. Being part of such a system has costs, though, and those costs go up with the level of danger. Belonging to a group that is dedicated to its own survival generally means pledging your life to it, which makes sense, because everyone else is pledging their life as well. Soldiers, firefighters, and criminal gangs are notorious for the ordeals they put novices through in order to find out who they can count on.

For those who pass the test, belonging to such a group can feel wildly liberating even though it must be one of the most oppressive forms of government ever devised.

That balancing act—a great freedom through an even greater loyalty—can be hard for people who have never been under serious threat to understand. Marginal groups such as motorcycle clubs and street gangs are drawn from threatened populations, however, so sacrifices make intuitive sense. And because these groups can be left very easily, authority tends to be bestowed from below rather than imposed from above. It's hard to be abusive or impose your will on someone who is there voluntarily. In that sense there is no *real* authority in marginal groups; there is mostly leadership by example and decision by consensus.

In the Lawndale part of Chicago's West Side, a street gang called the Vice Lords carved out fifty or sixty square blocks of home turf by putting these principles into effect in the 1960s. It was an exceedingly violent time in Chicago, and for many young black men, belonging to a gang that controlled territory was an obvious way to survive. A young anthropologist named Lincoln Keiser spent two summers with the Lords documenting how this was done. The Vice Lords initiation sometimes meant fighting everyone in the club at the same time, and membership was simply defined as joining any street fight that involved another Lord member, regardless of the odds. If you failed this simple test of loyalty, you risked being bundled into a car and dropped off in rival gang territory. What happened to you was your problem.

The reward for such loyalty was twofold: you were safe from other gangs and you had equality within your own. There was no seniority or special privilege within the Lords; leaders were those who could get others to follow them, and members were those who were willing to fight for the club. Any other metrics were considered a waste of time. Cheap wine had an almost ritual importance among the Vice Lords, and the way it was distributed reinforced the radical equality that kept the gang intact. Members would pool their money to buy a bottle, but every member got the same amount of wine regardless of how much—or little—he had contributed. And a first portion was always poured onto the sidewalk for Lords who were no longer there. Even death or imprisonment could not keep those men from benefiting from membership in the group.

In the morning we boiled creekwater for coffee and walked into the town of Newport on the first hot day of spring with steam rising off the roads and robins scrabbling in last year's leaves. Townspeople were in their yards tidying up and planting flowers and some of them smiled at us, but others just looked and kept looking. One guy finally waved us over with a varnished walking staff that he'd taken off a length of strangle-vine he'd found in the woods. He said he was a Vietnam vet and that he wanted to give us one of his staffs, but I told him we couldn't take anything from anyone except water and good advice. We headed back to the broad heat of the tracks and finally made a creek an hour later that came down off the ridges and curled into a little pool under some oaks and hemlocks. We drank our fill at the creek and then sat against our packs and ate and smoked and washed and after an hour we moved on because high clouds had piled in from the southeast and the sunlight suddenly had that flat pewter cast of oncoming rain.

We moved fast, only stopping when trains came through and we stepped into the brush and slash that bordered the tracks. We pushed past the old ferry station north of Newport and Reiders Run and Wildcat Run and passed through the breach at Wildcat Ridge. The weather finally caught us at Millerstown where Route 17 crosses the Juniata. We were sitting on our packs under the roadway when cold air came scuttling up the river. The rain arrived moments later, rattling the foliage and slatting across the water and smacking the top ballast. The overpass had been built above the buttresses of an old bridge, and after a while we crossed the tracks and climbed down the embankment until we sat behind the old quarrystone footing, which hid us from a few houses that were clustered along the road.

The rain eased off and eventually the world sat wet and subdued in the coming dusk. It was while we took a moment in the strange dry dust beneath the span that the shooting started, half a dozen cracks that whip-snapped over our heads and bounced around the empty acoustics of the overpass. One of us grabbed the machete and began a big looping circle to the right, trying to get behind whoever was shooting, while another man climbed the old bridge footing to peek over the top. The other two stayed where they were, waiting for the next volley, but that never came.

Five or six shots was probably someone emptying a revolver over our heads—it was a sharp little sound, like a .22—and the fact that we never saw him must have meant he ran away. A local who didn't like the way we crouched by our packs or some kid who needed a thrill. It was getting dark and we built a fire out of floodwrack and dead alder that hadn't been rained on since the overpass was built. The fire flared and then settled, and we set riverwater to boil and raked coals out to simmer onions and mushrooms and sausage in a pan. Traffic became more irregular and the sounds of town died down and we could hear the Juniata murmuring heavily alongside us. After dinner we brought our bowls and cookpots to the riverbank to wash and went to bed with spare clothing balled up under our heads and headlamps around our necks and knives in our boots where we could find them in the dark.

I didn't think the guy with the gun would come back, but even if he did, he'd have a fifty-pound mix-breed coming at him through the underbrush in the dark and then us after; forget it. I heard a grade crossing go off and then the long warning of an air horn: the last passenger train plowing toward us through the darkness. You could sleep through freight trains but there was no sleeping through a passenger train. They blew past with so much speed and energy that they seemed to suck the whole world in as they went—trees, towns, even the tracks themselves—before spitting it all back out with a whump of compressed air and clattering trucks. Occasionally you'd catch a child's face frozen in astonishment as they locked eyes with you before getting swept on up the tracks. Adults never seemed to look out the window long enough for that to happen, I thought. It was always the children who saw you.

Throughout history, good people and bad have maintained their freedom by simply staying out of reach of those who would deprive them of it. That generally meant walking a lot. Walking is the single cheapest, most reliable way of traveling without others knowing. Daniel Boone, the famed trapper and explorer, was known for going into the wilderness with little more than a rifle, a bedroll, and the clothes he was wearing. He and one or two companions would spend six months walking from Carolina to Kentucky and Tennessee, trapping as they went and returning home with packhorses loaded with furs. Once Boone went as far as Florida. He called these trips "Long Hunts." He'd be gone so long that his wife would take lovers and people would think he was dead, but he wasn't. He was doing what people have always done to make sure no one can tell them what to do or how to live their life.

Like Boone in enemy territory, most escaped slaves in the 1800s also maintained their freedom by walking. That meant keeping to the woods and uplands and sleeping cold and foraging for food. In 1849 a young slave named Charles Bell fled Romney, West Virginia, with his sixteen-year-old bride, Catherine, and headed north. "We walked thirty miles to the Potomac," he recounted to a journalist shortly before his death in 1912. "We made straight for the mountains, never stopping until we reached them. Rain had been falling all day. For a week it poured. . . . During the day we rested as best we could under some thick trees or overhanging rocks, and at night we travelled. As soon as it was dark, we worked our way down to the highway and all night long we stumbled along in the mud. . . . For four weeks we kept to the mountains. After we had been travelling a week or two, we came down to the highway but almost the first thing we saw was a poster, nailed to a dead tree, describing me and offering a reward for my return. We never again ventured on the highway in the daytime."

The Bells walked all the way to Pittsburgh, where they met a man who was an operative for the Underground Railroad, which smuggled escaped slaves to freedom. They moved to Niagara and were eventually put in a stagecoach to cross the bridge into Canada. In the middle of the span the driver turned around and said, "Now you are in Canada and as free as anybody."

A couple of generations after Boone opened up Kentucky, the U.S. government rounded up an estimated fifty thousand Choctaw, Seminole, Chickasaw, Muskogee, and Cherokee and marched them hundreds of miles to Oklahoma—the infamous "Trail of Tears." Some made the trip barefoot in midwinter, and mortality rates reached 25 percent. The exodus took years to complete, but a small group of Seminole managed to avoid removal by disappearing into the swamps of central Florida. Their tribal name was a corruption of the Spanish word *cimarron*, meaning "wild ones" or "runaways," because they had split off from the Creek Nation and emigrated southward a century earlier. They accepted anyone who showed up peacefully at their villages and thus became a haven for slaves who had escaped from white plantations in Alabama and Georgia.

In 1835 the U.S. government got serious about rounding up the remaining Seminole and sent roughly 5,000 federal troops into the Everglades to root them out. A few hundred Seminole and fugitive slaves fought them to a standstill, in one battle wiping out almost an entire company—107 men. After losing 1,500 soldiers and spending an estimated $30 million, the government finally gave up and left this renegade tribe in peace. Ten years later another round of fighting ended the same way. The descendants of these people continued in almost complete isolation until the 1930s, and they are the only indigenous group to have never signed a legal agreement with the United States.

All the other tribes were settled on reservations in the poorest areas of Oklahoma, but a few individuals managed to slip their military overseers and make it back to their homeland. A young Yuchi woman named Te-lah-nay was one of them, walking seven hundred miles from Oklahoma to northwestern Alabama, where she'd grown up. She later said that she had heard the great river of her childhood—the Tennessee—calling to her. She traveled alone, keeping to valleys until she saw white people and then retreating to the woods and high ridges. She lived off crawfish grabbed from streams and rabbits and squirrels caught in snares and fallow corn left in the fields. She was twice taken in by families but always resumed her journey and finally made it to the Devil's Backbone, an area of rugged hills south of the Tennessee River that she remembered from childhood. A few small groups of Chickasaw natives had managed to elude capture and remained hiding in this area as well. Te-lah-nay was taken in by a white family in the town of Tuscumbia, Alabama, and died a decade or so later, a respected member of the community.

For most of prehistory, humans lived in small groups that, like Te-lah-nay, traveled at a pace that allowed them to hunt and forage and didn't tire out the children. They rarely encountered other groups; their struggle was mostly with the natural world, not with each other. It was a hard but fairly egalitarian way of life that originated in Africa hundreds of thousands of years ago and eventually spread across Mesopotamia, Europe, Asia, and into North and South America via the Bering Strait.

The first sedentary communities were established around ten thousand years ago in Mesopotamia when Neolithic hunters began to plant wild grains like wheat and einkorn and barley. Farming requires an organized labor force but can support large numbers of people in a small area, and within several thousand years, massive population centers had sprung up. One of the first cities in the world, Uruk, had a huge standing army and as many as forty thousand people within its great walls. To hunters and shepherds, farming must have seemed unheroic and dull. To farmers, hunting must have just seemed like a gambit to avoid the hard work of tilling fields and digging irrigation ditches. Nomads tended to keep to marginal, rocky land that could never support crops, and one can imagine Neolithic farmers looking out at the dead mountains around them and being thankful that they passed their lives in one place and didn't have to continually search for food.

But one can also imagine—*easily* imagine—hunters and shepherds watching men plow fields in the hot sun and thinking that such a life was a kind of servitude, and that it was better to risk starving in the mountains than to eat well on the plains. "Nomadic movement of all types . . . is apparently not seen as a burdensome necessity but positively as something healthy and desirable in itself," writes anthropologist James Woodburn of hunter-gatherers. "Most important . . . is the way that such arrangements are subversive for the development of authority. Individuals are not bound to fixed areas . . . They are able to move away without difficulty and at a moment's notice. Adults of either sex can readily, if they choose, obtain enough food to feed themselves and are *potentially* autonomous."

Although wealthier and more stable, sedentary societies were often beset by an odd inferiority complex. In the biblical story of fratricide, Cain is the firstborn son who has inherited all of his father's agricultural land, and Abel is a wanderer who tends his flocks in the wilderness. But when it comes time to make a sacrifice to God, Cain can only offer vegetables, while Abel has a fat sheep. Consumed with jealousy, Cain kills his younger brother and leaves his body in a field. The Lord says that Abel's blood cries out from the soil for vengeance, and Cain will no longer be able to make his living from that soil. He must wander the Earth cursed among men rather than free among the animals, as Abel had been.

"The sedentary world always looked at the nomadic world with a combination of suspicion and envy," says nomadism scholar Paolo Ognibene. "The Greeks considered the surrounding people barbarians, but they also had the idea that they had a fair society and lived in contact with nature peacefully—a kind of proto-communism."

There doesn't seem to be much self-doubt among nomadic peoples, however—in fact, one may be able to gauge the value of freedom by the level of contempt with which mobile societies hold sedentary ones. *I do not have a mill with willow trees, I have a horse and whip, I will kill you and go,* Yomut tribesmen of northern Iran were fond of boasting. Mass societies have come to dominate the world by virtually every measure, but they require such high levels of obedience that sometimes even their own citizens balk. Once you have spent years digging irrigation ditches or picking stones out of a wheat field—or working at a law firm—you have almost no leverage with which to insist on your autonomy, or anyone else's. The choice is to either rise up or submit, and many hardworking people understandably choose to submit.

The sense of superiority often held by mobile societies stemmed in part from their warlike culture. "Nomads tend to have strong warrior traditions, in which young men who are initiated together . . . must protect their own herds and raid outside for animals," write scholars Allen Johnson and Timothy Earle. Sheep and cattle disperse across far too much land to be monitored, so herding societies often depend on a reputation for ferocity and revenge to keep people from stealing them. A wheat field is almost impossible to steal, so farming societies can afford to be much more docile.

The domestication of the horse only amplified this split. Mounted nomads such as Genghis Khan's "Mongol Horde" could move so quickly and attack so unexpectedly that even heavily fortified societies in China and Europe were at pains to defend themselves. And nomads had an intimate knowledge of the natural world that made them almost impossible to pursue and defeat. "Their traditional way of life necessitated a keen ability to understand animals, to navigate by stars, to read topography, to interpret the faces of strangers and to memorize oral literature," writes anthropologist Jack Weatherford. "And Eurasian nomads also imposed fewer social restraints on women, and even the highest leaders, such as Genghis Khan, explained away female infidelity and allowed the incorporation of children into families . . . no matter who fathered them."

The result was that nomadic society was far more appealing to the settled world than vice versa—particularly among the poor and disenfranchised. Chinese officials dismissed the Mongols as thieves and barbarians, but in truth, they had a hard time keeping their own citizens from fleeing to the steppe. Some scholars, including Weatherford, believe that the Great Wall of China was built as much to keep their own people in as to keep the "barbarians" out. The very qualities that made nomadism so alluring also made it incapable of governing well, however, and eventually a kind of stasis developed across Central Asia. Nomads roamed freely through land they could never really control, and settled societies controlled land they could never really leave. Empires paid nomads to not attack them, and nomads depended on empires for skills and trade goods that they could never develop on their own.

Still, nomads shooting recurved bows from nimble little steppe horses had an ability to terrify people that far exceeded their military prowess. In the sixth century BCE, King Darius I of Persia led the most powerful army of antiquity against the Scythians, a nomadic raiding culture at the edge of his empire. In military terms the Scythians didn't have a chance, but they didn't seem to know that. As the two armies faced each other across the battlefield, the Scythian warriors noticed hares in the underbrush and started hunting them. This act of insouciance so unnerved Darius that he withdrew his armies under cover of night.

"The Scythians weren't invincible, but their relationship with death was different," says Ognibene. "A Scythian fighter does not give up hunting a hare even if he is about to die—an incomprehensible thing for a Persian."

We were not nomadic horsemen, we were men on foot moving through a land designed for cars and trains, and it was easy to imagine we had nothing to do with the colossus around us. One night we were cooking dinner and a freight train thundered by with so much noise and power that I tossed out what I thought was an unanswerable question: What would it take to stop something like that instantaneously? I imagined some kind of massive wall, but the answer was more obvious: another train going just as fast in the opposite direction. America could seem like that as well, a country moving so fast and with so much weight that only a head-on collision with itself could make it stop.

Our insignificance alongside so much energy even started to feel like its own form of freedom until we realized that everything we needed—food, clothes, gear—came from the very thing we thought we were outwitting. If subsistence-level survival were the standard for absolute freedom, the word would mean nothing because virtually no one could pass that test. People love to believe they're free, though, which is hard to achieve in a society that has outsourced virtually all of the tasks needed for survival. Few people grow their own food or build their own homes, and no one—literally no one—refines their own gasoline, performs their own surgery, makes their own ball bearings, grinds their own eyeglass lenses, or manufactures their own electronics from scratch. Everyone—including people who vehemently oppose any form of federal government—depend on a sprawling supply chain that can only function with federal oversight, and most of them pay roughly one-third of their income in taxes for the right to participate in this system.

For most of human history, freedom had to be at least suffered for, if not died for, and that raised its value to something almost sacred. In modern democracies, however, an ethos of public sacrifice is rarely needed because freedom and survival are more or less guaranteed. That is a great blessing but allows people to believe that any sacrifice at all—rationing water during a drought, for example—are forms of government tyranny. They are no more forms of tyranny than rationing water on a lifeboat. The idea that we can enjoy the benefits of society while owing nothing in return is literally infantile. Only children owe nothing.

To be fair, it's hard to feel loyalty to a society that is so huge it hardly even knows we're here and yet makes sure we are completely dependent on it. That's not a strong bargaining position for the individual to be in. Wealth is supposed to liberate us from the dangers of dependency but quickly becomes a dependency in its own right. The wealthier we are, the higher our standard of living and the more—not less—we depend on society for our safety and comfort. On the outskirts of D.C., we met a man who was walking along holding a box turtle he'd found in a creek. He said he was going to sell it to a pet store, but he was on foot and the nearest store was three miles away. That was an hour's walk each way. Was he more or less free than people who work all day to make payments on a car every month?

Poverty is its own cruel trap but still raises questions about whether we own our possessions or are owned by them. Somewhere in the middle of Pennsylvania we saw a man who had tied the handle of a snow shovel to his belt and then piled all his belongings onto the blade, which sledded along behind him. Depending on your perspective he was either the freest man in the country or just the poorest.

When Francisco Vázquez de Coronado, the Spanish explorer, first encountered the endless grasslands of Texas in 1541, his Indian scouts returned from a reconnaissance mission to report that in sixty miles, "they had seen nothing but buffalo and sky." The European mind was unprepared for such vastness. Coronado marched 1,500 men, 1,000 horses, and 500 head of cattle over plains that at times threatened to swallow them whole. "They left no more trace than if no one had passed over," wrote the expedition's chronicler, Pedro de Castañeda. "It became necessary to stack up piles of bones and dung so that the rear guard could follow the army and not get lost."

There were two kinds of Natives in this strange land: those who slept in stone or adobe houses and those who slept in tents or under nothing at all. The wealthiest and most sophisticated tribes had fortified towns, called pueblos, that sat atop mesas and were virtually impregnable. The Pueblo peoples cultivated corn and squash and beans and worked silver that they set with turquoise and were known for their exquisite baskets and fine, thin-walled pottery. When they

were threatened, they generally withdrew to their fortifi-
cations and taunted their attackers from above. They rolled
boulders off the ramparts and fought from rooftops and
alleys and made conquest so costly that few tried it.

Until the Spaniards showed up. According to Castañeda,
Coronado's men took Hawikuh, the western-most of the Zuni
pueblos, in less than an hour. At the Hopi town of Tusayan,
inhabitants just rushed forward with gifts so that the Spaniards
would show mercy on them. Acoma fell quickly even though
it rode 350 feet above the surrounding plain on a mesa that
was so steep, it could only be gained by ladders. And the powerful, wealthy pueblo of Tiguex fought through the winter of
1540–41 but fell after the Tewa defenders were smoked out
with smudge fires and promised mercy if they surrendered.
Instead, the Spaniards tied two hundred Tewa men to stakes
and burned them alive as a warning to other pueblos. Seeing
this, the remainder tried to fight their way through the Spanish
cordon but were cut down almost to a man.

Far more successful at defying the Spaniards—and
everyone else—were the small, mobile bands of Apache
hunters that lived in the same area. (The name means "our
enemy" in Zuni.) Coronado first encountered them on the
plains of west Texas, where he came upon an encampment
of "Querechos," as he called them—probably Lipan Apache.
To his amazement, these people neither got out of the way

nor showed much deference at the approach of his huge army. They were a wild, fearless people who were perfectly adapted to their environment. They slept in buffalo-skin tents and ate almost nothing but buffalo meat and made buffalo-intestine canteens, which they filled with blood and looped around their necks. Their all-meat diet predisposed them to scurvy, but they prevented that by drinking the stomach contents of dead buffalo, which was mostly digested grasses that were high in vitamin C. Afoot in an immense land, they were still able to give Coronado's scouts a detailed description of the Mississippi River, which lay five hundred miles to the east. "These Indians left this place the following day," Castañeda reported, "droves of dogs carrying their belongings."

Spanish horsemen strapped into armor and backed by cannon might successfully besiege a Pueblo town, but they couldn't hope to run down small bands of Apache in the mountains. It was the very poverty of the Apache—nothing to defend and almost nothing to carry—that made them hard to subdue, and therefore free. An encampment of Chiricahua Apache could start mobilizing in minutes and move faster than cavalry in rugged terrain. They poisoned water sources with coyote intestines as they fled and raided white settlements for supplies and fresh horses and splintered into even smaller groups when cornered. "They scatter like quail and meet again at some distant point previously understood," one American general complained three centuries later. "It is exceedingly difficult for our troops to overtake and punish them."

Scattering like quail allowed the Apache to remain autonomous almost until the age of the airplane and automobile. While their wealthy Pueblo neighbors were being tortured, killed, and enslaved by the missionaries and conquistadores, the Apache roamed the same area unimpeded. While the Navajo were being rounded up and force-marched three hundred miles to an internment camp in the 1860s, the Apache were raiding deep into Mexico for horses, livestock, and weapons. While almost a million workers were launching the first nationwide labor strikes in American cities in the 1880s, the last free Apache were trying to decide whether it was better to die fighting or surrender to the federal government.

American cavalry had a hard time catching even Apache civilians, much less the warriors themselves. Children slept with pouches of food tied to their bodies so they could flee in the middle of the night and still have something to eat. Girls performed hard labor and trained on weapons just like the boys so they could run or fight, as circumstances required. If a band of Apache was in danger of being overtaken by U.S. cavalry, older warriors stayed with the women and children while the young fighters went out to deal with the enemy. They rode the best horses and carried the best guns but moved slowly, as if encumbered by dependents, and the Americans invariably assumed they had cornered the entire group. In fact, the women and children were fleeing by another route while the warriors toyed with their pursuers.

On raids, Apache warriors kept to the mountains during the day and waited until dark to cross the plains. From the high peaks they could see American cavalry sixty or seventy miles away because of the dust they raised. They cut telegraph wires between towns and spliced them back together with rawhide so the cuts would be hard to find. According to the famed war chief Geronimo, they moved forty-five miles a day on foot and were expected to be able to put away seventy if necessary. On the way back from raids they often walked and ran nonstop for several days straight. "I was on foot like a great many of us were," one Apache warrior explained to anthropologist Grenville Goodwin in the 1930s, "but in those days my legs were like automobiles."

Apache raiders carried little more than weapons and dried food and limited their clothing to moccasins and a breechclout, or an odd assemblage of Western castoffs. A chief known as Mangas Coloradas—"Colored Sleeves"— wore a checkered shirt, blue overalls cut off at the knee, and a white straight-brim sombrero. Their weapons were simple and weighed so little that warriors could easily run with them. A few men carried sotol-wood lances tipped with bayonets or saber blades, and everyone else carried bows or pistols and even lever-action carbines. The bows were made from wild mulberry and strung with deer sinew that was nocked to a reed arrow fletched with hawk feathers and tipped with flint or hoop iron, often poisoned. The bows were short and powerful and could drive an arrow through a man or deer and "almost through a man standing sideways," according to Goodwin.

War leaders were simply men who inspired trust in other men, and the Apache word for leader could be roughly translated as "dew trampler," because they walked in front of everyone else and literally shook the dew off vegetation as they passed. A good leader was considered the tactical equivalent of twelve men, and his comrades showed him respect by not allowing him to do any camp work while on a raid. During peacetime, however, a war leader was an ordinary person with no special privileges. A succession of such leaders kept American authorities off balance for decades, easily passing through farm and ranchland and raiding at will from Colorado to central Mexico. In the summer of 1881, a Chiricahua leader named Nana led a small group of warriors on a raid that covered 1,500 miles in six weeks.

They defeated or evaded more than a thousand American troops, killed as many as fifty American civilians, captured two hundred head of horses and mules, and made it safely back to their refuge in the Mexican sierra. Nana was thought to be at least seventy-five years old.

Geronimo was the last Native war leader of the American continent. He gave himself up at a place called Skeleton Canyon, Arizona, in 1886, after a year on the run in the Mexican sierra. By then the light bulb, the telephone, the four-stroke engine, and the machine gun had all been invented. Geronimo had only a dozen warriors with him at the end—the rest of his group were women and children—and it had taken four troops of cavalry and scores of Navajo and Apache scouts to corner him. The Apache were relieved of their guns and animals and put on a train for Florida, and their dogs and horses chased them for miles as the train clattered eastward. From Florida they were moved to other southern states and eventually to Fort Sill, Oklahoma, where many of the tribal reservations were located. Geronimo died of pneumonia in 1909 after falling off his horse and laying outside all night. He may have been drunk. According to Geronimo's nephew, his last words were, "I should have fought until I was the last man left alive."

That honor belonged to a Yahi man known as Ishi, who walked out of the chaparral-choked canyons of Mount

Lassen, California, in 1911. He was emaciated and wrapped in a scrap of covered-wagon canvas and had collapsed at a slaughterhouse outside the small town of Oroville. The butchers were woken at dawn by dogs barking and went outside to find Ishi cowering in a corral. They called the local sheriff on a telephone and told him they were holding a "wild man," and Sheriff J. B. Webber and his deputies showed up with their guns drawn.

Ishi was the last member of his tribe. He was born in the early 1860s, during an era of horrific attacks and counterattacks that almost wiped out the Yahi population. In one massacre, thirty-three Yahi men, women, and children were cornered in a cave at Campo Seco, near Mill Creek, and shot to pieces by a posse of local men. (The killers reportedly exchanged their Spencer rifles for revolvers because even they couldn't stomach the damage done by large-caliber bullets to the human body—particularly to the children.) A dozen or so Yahi escaped into the upper reaches of Deer Creek Canyon and began what was later described by anthropologists as "the long concealment." Ishi was six or seven years old. For more than three decades, this little group hunted with bow and arrow, camouflaged their camps with branches, cooked over twig fires, traveled by leaping from boulder to boulder to avoid leaving tracks, and crawled through heavy chaparral where no white man would ever think to look.

As Ishi grew into a man his little group died off until only he, his mother, his sister, and his grandfather remained. One day the family scattered at the approach of some white men, and Ishi never saw his sister and grandfather again. (They may have drowned trying to escape across a creek.) Ishi's mother died soon after, and Ishi made it another three years before giving up. He was alone, starving, and had no reason to live. He walked out of Deer Creek Canyon expecting to be killed by the first white person he saw and went another forty miles before coming to a stop at the slaughterhouse outside Oroville. Ishi was taken to the local jail, and anthropologist T. T. Waterman hurried from the University of California at Berkeley by train to try to communicate with him.

Waterman eventually brought him back to Berkeley, where he was named "Ishi"—the Yahi word for "man"—after he refused to reveal his tribal name. A Berkeley anthropologist named Alfred Kroeber took him under his wing and began to document his extraordinary skills. Ishi was eventually hired as a janitor at the university and began teaching members of the anthropology department to chip flint, make bows and arrows, start a fire without matches, and hunt rabbit and deer. He was, by some definitions, the last completely free person in North America, and it bears noting that even with his lifetime of wilderness skills, Ishi could not—physically and emotionally—keep himself alive without the help of others. He died of tuberculosis in 1916, at age fifty-five. His last words, reportedly, were, "You stay, I go."

Small groups like the Yahi and Apache tend to protect themselves by staying on the move and large groups tend to protect themselves by digging in and fighting. Small groups fight when cornered, of course, and on the frontier, there was thought to be nothing more dangerous than a wounded Apache trying to give the rest of his band time to escape. But it was the Apache's ability to cross terrain quickly and invisibly that allowed fourteen generations to remain outside the control of white society. If this were not so—if large, powerful groups were just as agile and hard to detect as small ones—they would win every conflict and dominate every society.

But they don't. The cost of cornering and killing determined resistors in virtually any environment—city, desert, mountain, jungle—is so high that large-scale societies often give up. None of this would be possible without the singular human ability to move huge distances on foot. Other primates can't come close to matching human performance on the ground, and even horses, dogs, and wolves have trouble outrunning humans in steep terrain or hot weather.

The Western States 100, in which runners and horseback riders race one hundred miles over the Sierra Nevada, sees humans and horses running roughly similar times.

(Runners and riders compete separately but on almost identical courses.) The record for runners, fourteen hours and nine minutes, was set by ultramarathoner Jim Walmsley in 2019. Walmsley covered the distance almost two hours faster than the fastest horse-and-rider entrant that year and would have beaten all but one of the horse-and-rider entrants over the previous twenty years. Many animals sprint faster than humans, but few can compare across such a range of distances—especially in the heat. Top male runners can maintain a pace of around twenty mph for a quarter mile; fifteen mph for three miles; and ten mph for fifty miles. (Three-minute-mile pace, four-minute-mile pace, and six-minute-mile pace, respectively.) The world record for one hundred miles is well under twelve hours, and humans are able to keep up that level of performance for days on end. In 1988, a Greek runner named Yiannis Kouros set the thousand-mile world record by running 144 miles on the first day and going on to cover the full distance in ten days and ten hours, a record that still stands.

Almost all running distances have a gender performance gap of around 11 percent, which is much lower than it is for weight events. From bench press to javelin to the discus to hammer throw, female athletes perform at roughly 50 to 70 percent of the level of male athletes. The discrepancy is due to the fact that, starting in utero, men have much higher testosterone levels than women, giving them almost twice the upper body strength. Chromosomal differences between the sexes also produce distinct morphologies which cannot be undone with supplemental hormone injections. Long-distance running is far less determined by testosterone than strength events, so the gender discrepancy is lower. In evolutionary terms, it may have been more adaptive for women to keep up with their men rather than fight alongside them. The sexual division of labor is a human universal, and in every society, women perform the majority of childcare, and men perform the majority of group defense. Changing that dynamic may well promote greater freedom and equality, but throughout human history, women's ability to run long distances means that entire communities could be on the move without sorting by gender and the tactical problems that would create.

One of the adaptations that makes such endurance feats possible, psychologically, is the ability to experience time and effort in a variety of ways. Exertion causes the brain to release endorphins that mask pain and are mildly narcotic, and the repetitive nature of running or walking can lull the mind into a kind of hypnosis. Young children fall asleep very quickly in the arms of someone who is walking, or in anything—like a mechanical rocker—that mimics the human gait. An athlete who is deeply locked into a long-distance cadence can cover ten or twenty miles without seeming to expend much effort; in such a state, running can feel almost as easy as walking or riding a bicycle.

And the body does not decline at a steady rate during all-day runs but rather goes through cycles of discomfort, agony, and something bordering on intoxication. That means that however much a runner might be struggling, a mile from now—or twenty miles—she might be feeling great again. Courtney Dauwalter is one of the best ultramarathoners in the world and has won several races outright—both male and female divisions. Dauwalter's longest run is 279 miles, which she completed in sixty-seven hours. She believes she can run four hundred. She has run all night and been surprised by how far she has gone; and she has run a mile and been stunned by how hard it was. Daybreak often brings a temporary sense of optimism and energy, and nighttime can bring the opposite: fatigue and depression and even hallucinations. Some hallucinations are actually dreams that occur when the mind grabs moments of sleep during the run.

"I've seen a leopard in a hammock," Dauwalter says. "A guy playing a cello. One time there was a colonial woman, and a cowboy with a big yellow bucket-hat twirling his rope. And once there were white cats all over the trail. I was trying not to step on them."

Fit people obviously outperform unfit ones, but their minds are also better adapted to stress. A study from 2012 put three groups—U.S. Marines, elite athletes, and "ordinary" people—into fMRIs and gradually reduced their oxygen supply. While this was happening, the subjects performed cognitive tests. MRIs are loud, intimidating machines that often trigger claustrophobia, and having one's air supply reduced in such a situation would add enormously to the stress. As expected, the control group performed worse on the cognitive tests as their air supply dwindled, but the Marines and elite athletes performed *better*. Their minds responded to the threatening stimuli by focusing even more intently on the task at hand. In societies like the Apache that expect almost everyone to run or walk all day long, this elite response to stress might be so widespread as to be utterly unremarkable.

I opened my eyes to the thud of car tires hitting the spacers above us. We sacked our gear and laced our boots and headed downtrack on cobble that rolled out from underfoot and made us feel clumsy and inexperienced. A work crew west of town forced us down into the river bracken and we picked our way along deer trails for half a mile before pulling ourselves back up the embankment to the tracks. From time to time we passed cornfields wedged into little gores of flatland between the ridges and quarrystone or clapboard houses that were built before the Civil War and had big pleasant verandas hanging off their fronts.

We passed a deer exploded across the tracks as if by dynamite, a reminder for us in case we needed one. The river now ran straight along the base of Tuscarora Mountain past the remnants of Durward Station and Thompsontown and Vandyke. Freight trains passed every twenty minutes with the engineers waving if we waved first, so we didn't even bother trying to hide. One freight passed us with a mile of brightly painted Japanese tractors stacked on flatbeds headed west and another passed with a mile of Humvees and Bradleys and M1s on flatbeds headed east. Turrets empty and tank barrels cocked down. The country opened up after Port Royal, and we made camp in a little floodplain where the river broadens and runs so sluggishly that you could consider swimming on a hotter day. Plenty of deadwood in the floodwrack and big sycamores and hickories and maples to provide cover from the scattering of nice houses across the river.

Mifflintown lay a few miles ahead so the next morning we walked straight into town and left our dog tied to our packs outside a little diner. We squeezed into a booth and ordered great plates of pancakes and bacon and eggs and home fries. While we ate we took turns shaving and brushing our teeth in the little bathroom and if the owner minded he didn't say anything. There were local men at the counter—farmers by the looks of them—and one of them was ageless and strong and stubborn-looking in his cap and jeans. He turned to study us and said he'd fought in World War Two and then turned back to his meal without another word.

We filled our water bottles and filed out of the little diner, each of us thanking the entire room, old heads nodding as the door banged behind us. Most of the storefronts were shuttered so we stepped onto the rail lines without worrying about anyone calling the cops and just set forth. Adjust the belt, adjust the straps, adjust the stride until you've found that familiar all-day rhythm that is more of a forward-rolling motion than a walk and feels at least bearable if not, occasionally, unstoppable.

A few miles outside Mifflintown the river bends west again at Lewistown Narrows, where the waters squeeze between Shade Mountain and Blue Mountain. Everywhere we looked the slopes bore the scars of ancient rockslides and brushfires and dropped almost straight into the river. We kicked a level spot out of the dirt to sit on and set a discarded tie plate on top of two rocks for a grill and then built a fire underneath. When the steel was hot enough to spit oil we dropped beefsteaks onto it that we'd gotten earlier in the day and flipped them with the tips of our knives while we cooked corn tortillas on the side. We ate everything with our hands and our knives, tossing the gristle to the dog and then wiping our hands down on pants that already seemed filthier than anything our hands could offer.

Freights rumbled back and forth above us on the tracks and cars passing along Route 22 across the river sounded like distant surf. Someone shot a rifle out of a passing truck. We'd each dug our own beds out of the slope so we could sleep without rolling into the river and we were strung along the bank like linked sausages. The fire embers still pulsed, and the night air was soft and benevolent, and it felt like summer waited for us a few days upriver. My dog lay on my ankles, and the three other men shifted and muttered next to me in their sleep. There may be better things than that, but not many.

BOOK TWO · FIGHT

The first white immigrants into the Juniata spoke little if any English and knew no more about the wilderness than what could be transposed from rural life in Europe. They were Dutch and German and Swiss and finally the notorious Scotch-Irish, who were sometimes exempted from paying land fees in exchange for settling remote areas where they might serve as a buffer for civilization. These people threaded their way up the Juniata singly and in small groups and threw up log shelters that could at least stop arrows and get them through the first winter. The chimneys were made from logs as well, plastered with clay, and settlers left ropes dangling from the top so the whole stack could be pulled over if it caught fire and threatened the rest of the building.

The country was shale and sandstone and limestone occasionally shot through with volcanic trapp. Limestone erodes easily and is more fertile than shale, so limestone valleys were prized for the rich crops they produced. Before colonial authority reached the frontier, land claims were established by blazing trees with an ax and then carving one's initials into the bark. "Tomahawk rights," as they were called, had no legal standing, but newcomers paid cash for them rather than risk conflicts with the men who were already there.

The American frontier was already a place of almost mythic freedom and possibility, and the Juniata led straight to the heart of it. Early settlers learned how to make ink out of gunpowder and horse bridles out of hickory bark and gunflints out of arrowheads that could be found by the hundreds at ancient campsites. They melted pewter spoons and plates into bullets during Indian attacks and used the same medicinal herbs as the Natives and performed the same rude surgery: digging bullets and arrowheads out of flesh with hot knives and applying poultices so that the person didn't die of infection.

Hunting was crucial to frontier survival but so alluring that it was often hard to keep the men focused on farm work. Boys learned to shoot by ten or twelve and grew to dress like Indians in deerskin leggings and loose hunting shirts that were belted around the waist so that the entire thing could serve as a big pouch. In went the beef jerky, the hunks of bread, the hominy cakes, and the oilcloth for greasing the rifle. They shot small-bore muzzleloaders of German design that could hit a man at several hundred yards but required an inhuman calm during battle. Reloading meant pouring a measure of powder down the barrel, following that with a lead ball patched with oilcloth, driving it home with a ramrod, tapping more powder into the pan, and then snapping the frizzen shut. The guns were accurate because they were long—up to six feet—and some men learned how to reload them at a dead run.

There was little chance a lone family could fight off the Indians with such slow-loading weapons, so messengers known as "expresses" raced from cabin to cabin to warn remote homesteads that an attack was coming. Expresses often arrived in the middle of the night, rapping on the door or window and then moving on. Terrified settlers straggled into the outforts and stockades all night long, some still wearing their bedclothes. Women carried infants and men carried older children, and any child too heavy to carry simply had to walk. Some families had already survived an attack and arrived bloody and mute, having just witnessed loved ones tomahawked and scalped.

"On the fifth day of July, 1763, the Indians came to Juniata, it being harvest time, and the white people were come back to reap their crops," remembered a survivor named Robert Robison. "It was on the Sabbath Day; the reapers were all in the house. The Indians crept up nigh to the door and killed William White and all his family excepting one boy, who leapt out the window and made his escape." It was almost impossible to stop such attacks, and when settlers counterattacked, the combat was still desperate and disorganized. During one battle, a teenage boy named John Elliot managed to reload his rifle at a run and turn and shoot an Indian who was just steps behind him, tomahawk raised. The man fell to the ground clutching his stomach and Elliot kept going, passing a neighbor who was "weltering in his own blood." Elliot eventually made it back to his fort.

Frontier forts were log palisades constructed with little if any metal and not much better than what the Indians had. Some had blockhouses on the corners and gunloops every few feet and others were just heavily built cabins that could accommodate five or six families at most. Boys over the age of thirteen were considered "fort soldiers" and given rifles to shoot out the gunloops. The girls and women cared for the wounded and helped reload the rifles and put out fires that Indians sometimes managed to ignite in the roof shakes. And the men stood at the walls or in the blockhouses shooting through the gunloops or downward over the top to kill Indians who were trying to breach the palisade. Many kept pistols in their belts for close combat and stocked their cabins with axes and mattocks and hoes in case the fight moved indoors, where the children were.

They fought to the death because the consequences of losing were beyond contemplating. One settler was found in a thicket shot, tomahawked, and scalped but with his hands full of another man's hair that he must have pulled out during the fight. Most men were tomahawked on the spot, but some were marched back to the village to provide the entertainment of torture. A few were adopted if they were good shots and could help with hunting and fighting. Young women were adopted as well but tomahawked immediately if they couldn't keep up with the raiders on the way back. And if they tried to escape, they were tortured to death like the men, the honors often going to the women of the tribe. "First, they scalped her," a German woman testified about another captive. "Next, they laid burning splinters of wood upon her body. Then they cut off her ears and fingers, forcing them into her mouth so that she had to swallow them."

Life in populated areas farther east was brutally rigid—the most common civil offense was "contempt for authority"—and many settlers simply wanted to escape the scrutiny of church and state. Freedom on the frontier was a kind of mirage, though: the closer you got, the more danger you were in and the more you needed your neighbors for survival, which just meant obeying their rules rather than the government's. Freedom and safety seemed to exist on a continuum where the more you had of one, the less you had of the other. "There was neither law nor gospel," recounts an early settler named Joseph Doddridge about frontier society. "In a sparce population, where all the members of the community are known to each other and every man capable of bearing arms is considered highly valuable, public opinion has its full effects and answers the purposes of legal government."

Any man who refused to help fight was shunned by the community; even failing to carry a rifle and tomahawk was cause for censure. If such a man were not yet married, there was little chance he ever would be. Theft was judged by a "jury of the neighborhood," which usually imposed a sentence of flogging and banishment, and women who spoke ill of others were informed that they could say whatever they wanted but would never again be believed on any matter whatsoever. And unresolvable conflicts between men were usually settled with fistfights that had no rules other than prohibitions against weapons and eye-gouging. Once the fight was over, both men usually shook hands and forgot their differences; no one knew, day to day, who they might find themselves crouched next to during an Indian attack.

The Iroquois eventually sold off everything west of the Endless Mountains, and by 1790, the last Shawnee and Delaware had been pushed over the Alleghenies and the great land lay open to settlement. Whites quickly carved up the rich limestone valleys that intersected the Juniata: the Licking and the Kishacoquillas and Lost Creek Valley and the long, broad Tuscarora. The standing stone of the Onojutta-Haga was long gone, however, probably carried off by the Delaware when they first evacuated the valley. It is not known how they moved something that heavy, or why, but they clearly didn't want it falling into white hands. The stone has never been found.

We walked out of Lewistown Narrows on a hot April day and the terrain laid down as it ran west until the Alleghenies were just a distant presence at the edges of the farmland. From a hilltop we could see where they would close back in again but for now the Juniata just drew big wide meanders through the cornfields and river bottom. The rail lines had an ample maintenance road and trestles a hundred yards wide that meant we didn't have to worry about what was bearing down on us while we crossed the river. It was flat open country with plenty of firewood and drinking water and innumerable places to sleep even if you just stopped and lay down where you were. The lines ran secant across a big riverbend outside Lewistown and then ploughed westward past Granville and Anderson and finally a scattering of houses named Mattawana where we lay down in some underbrush by the river and went to sleep.

We were moving before people woke up in their houses

and the country was easy passage now, small towns miles apart and farmland almost to the horizon. Trains slammed past every half hour, Norfolk Southern, Intermodal, Hamburg Süd, Clipper, and we didn't even bother hiding from them. The quantity of what America needed was hard to comprehend: three straight minutes of cattle cars lumbering by with their barnyard stench, a mile of double-stacked connexes coming out of Newark and Philly, endless coal trains like a special delivery from hell. A trackside cross marked the spot where a teenager lost his life some years prior. We walked all day and made Mount Union in the early evening and walked down a deserted main street that must have been a hundred yards wide in a town that couldn't have had three thousand people. There was a restaurant at the edge of town with one cook and one waitress and no customers and we walked in with our packs and our dog and no one said a word. The waitress was young and asked when we were coming back through and one of us said never, why don't you join us? And she laughed and took our order and we were back up on the rail by nightfall.

There was almost no moon but underfoot was packed cinder that we could easily walk with headlamps or even no light at all. We walked Jack's Narrows at night passing Mapleton and Birdville as they slept and crossed back over the Juniata after Smith's Run where the river jags north.

Jack Armstrong was a trader who was killed by Indians in the winter of 1744; a search party reported finding nothing but his "shoulderbone." We chose our stopping place poorly in the dark and woke before dawn in a foul weed patch and made a breakfast of peanut butter and cold coffee and set out for Huntingdon. That was where the original standing stone had been; that was the center of the Onojutta-Haga world. There was a café at Huntingdon Station with outdoor tables that had a few people at them waiting for an eastbound Amtrak and we walked right in off the tracks and sat down. We'd moved forty miles in forty hours and felt like wolves. We ordered coffees and a plateful of whatever pastries they had and bagels with cream cheese toasted and wrapped in wax paper and when we couldn't eat any more we stood ourselves back up on leg muscles that had already set like concrete and hoisted our packs and moved on.

The river shot a gorge above Huntingdon that breached another ridge, which ran dead straight past the Potomac almost to the Shenandoah. It was still remote, inaccessible country that could only be reached by boat. From time to time we passed someone's fishing camp, usually a tent or tarpaper shack that sat just above flood stage with a spring-shot armchair or couch moldering in front of a firepit. A skiff tethered out front if anyone was home, working back and forth in the current like a dog with something wrong with it. The river hooked south at Petersburg and finally crossed a broad floodplain that had corn and wheatfields on either side. The mountains rose up again but were easily breached at Barree, and there were clean sweet creeks coming off the uplands and no houses or people to speak of who might notice our passing.

The weather backed around to the northeast and we made camp on a steep little hill above a cold spring that welled straight out of the rock. It was Saturday and we could hear cars and trucks gunning along 453 on the other side of the river. We were always worried about the locals and on a weekend night it seemed like a good idea to sleep at a place that was hard to find and easy to leave. If they came up one side, we'd go down the other. If that didn't work, we'd stay on top and see how badly they wanted this. We made a hot little fire of dead spruce and cooked enchiladas on a flat piece of railroad steel and went to sleep under our tarp before the rains came tapping in for the night.

Sometimes we could find a perfect place to sleep within sight of a suburban development—we'd use the red filter on our headlamps so no one would see us—and sometimes, wide-open country would give us nothing but rocks and corn stubble. South of Havre de Grace we walked half the night without finding a good spot and finally lay down on top ballast just feet from the rails themselves. We were so close we could hear the steel ringing before the big freights blew through. Each one was so catastrophically loud that in our half-sleep we were sure it had jumped the tracks or was coming down some rail spur we'd mistakenly bedded down on. In the morning one guy sat up and said, "I'd rather be mortared," which was something he knew about because he'd once caught some metal in his elbow during a firefight in Afghanistan.

There were countless ways to get killed, and sleeping on the trackbed was definitely one of them. Drunks and suicides and teenagers with headphones get hit all the time between the rails but there are less obvious dangers as well. Metal strapping can come unlimbered from its load and perform a kind of spastic dance alongside a moving train that will cut you in half. Steel wheels going 140 and bearing many tons of weight can shoot chunks of rock sideways off the rails like bullets. Cargo dangles and flails and falls from cars; an engineer was almost killed by a piece of timber that worked loose from its load and came straight through his cab from an oncoming train. He survived by dropping like a boxer under a right cross.

The towns, the cops, the freight companies—no one wanted us on the lines, which is understandable. In fact, over the course of four hundred miles, we failed to come up with a single moral or legal justification for what we were doing other than the dilute principle that we weren't causing actual harm so we should be able to keep doing it. The best way to not get caught was to not be seen, and most of the time, that was surprisingly easy. If you hear a train, step into the underbrush. If you're walking up on an overpass or grade crossing, put the binoculars on it to make sure no one in uniform is waiting for you. If there's nowhere to hide when a train comes through, wave at the engineer. If he doesn't wave back, assume he's going to call you in. If he calls you in, hide in the woods and smoke a cigarette or boil some coffee until the cops roll past. If the cops roll past in one direction, they're going to roll back in the other. If an hour goes by and they still haven't come, you can take your chances and step back onto the rail, or you can wait until dark. Then you can do whatever you want because everything that moves faster than you out there must use headlights, and those can be seen a mile out.

There are disadvantages to moving three miles an hour in a world that's mostly going seventy or eighty but there are also advantages. You can hide virtually anywhere and will probably see everyone else before they see you. Your largest vulnerability is someone coming from behind, but you can have everyone glance backward regularly on their own initiative. That kind of random surveillance is almost impossible to defeat. We got good at staying out of sight but still had our close calls. A day south of Wilmington, a maintenance crew rolled up on us from behind and the foreman told us to get off the tracks. Twenty minutes later, we watched from the woods as two Amtrak cops churned past in an SUV. We paralleled the tracks slowly through the woods for the rest of the day and then made up our mileage at night.

And one night north of Baltimore we were walking late to avoid the heat and suddenly the darkness was filled with lights and sirens and the heavy *whap whap whap* of a helicopter at low altitude. There wasn't much we could do but crouch down in tall grass and hope they didn't have infrared. We watched a cone of light wobble toward us and then pass within a hundred feet before continuing on up the line. It came back later to rerun its grid but by then we'd laid back and gone to sleep. We got up a couple of hours later and hoisted our bags and staggered off like exhausted drunks. We didn't know how much trouble we were in but wanted to make sure we were outside their search grid before people were back at their desks in the morning.

By definition everyone we met on railroad property was breaking the law, so they tended to be either very friendly or very guarded. Once we saw a guy step off the trackbed when he spotted us and carefully fit a pair of gloves onto his hands. He then pulled something out of his rucksack and slid it into his back pocket and dropped the ruck on the ground and waited. He gave himself as much standoff as possible and stood watching us carefully and not smiling. His right hand stayed by his waist and his left hand held a three-foot length of rebar with a U-shaped fixture welded to the bottom. We stopped to talk so he wouldn't think we'd seen his gun and he said he was a snake catcher and this was his snake iron and he walked the lines every day looking for snakes.

He didn't say what he did with them or how he made a living from it and I didn't ask. He added that he was new in town and that if he packed up and disappeared overnight no one would even notice, which I took to be a warning. I said goodbye, and when we were out of pistol range I turned to look and he was still standing there with his snake iron, staring.

The railroad lines we followed were there because that's where the settler roads had been, and the settler roads were there because that's where the Indian trails had been, and the Indian trails were there because—250 million years ago—the Juniata River had sawed her way through the shale and lime-stone strata of that country faster than tectonic forces could lift them up. Harder stone, such as granite, diverts rivers and creates barriers that people generally have to go around. The

Juniata offered a way through the Allegheny Front that had no viable alternative for hundreds of miles. The southern option went up the Potomac River and through the mountains of West Virginia; the northern option went by canal from upstate New York to Lake Erie.

The United States of the early 1800s, when the first railroads were built, had a relatively small population and very little capital. In order to compete with Europe, the federal government faced the prospect of spending a huge amount of money on infrastructure; otherwise, the new democracy would remain an economic backwater that was fatally divided between a thriving East Coast and an inaccessible interior. Transporting a bushel of wheat three hundred miles from Pittsburgh to Philadelphia cost more than the wheat was worth at market, and America's rugged geography was something that private enterprise couldn't hope to conquer on its own.

To solve the problem, America's Swiss-born treasury secretary, Albert Gallatin, proposed a massive infrastructure plan that would subsidize a network of roads and canals linking cities like Baltimore and Philadelphia with the Ohio River Valley. Although the plan was not passed, most of the projects Gallatin proposed in 1808 were eventually built, including a crucial rail and canal route up the Juniata. America's wealth and hegemony can be traced in part to

Gallatin's efforts to overcome his new country's aversion to federal investment and espouse a grander vision. A statue of Gallatin stands at the northern entrance of the Treasury Building in Washington, DC.

Twenty years after Gallatin's proposal, the inaugural spadeful of earth for a subsidized national railroad was turned by a man named Charles Carroll, who was the last surviving signatory of the Declaration of Independence. Carroll claimed to be prouder of the Baltimore and Ohio Railroad than of the historic document he'd signed, believing that a national transportation system—coupled with America's vast resources and almost unlimited immigrant and slave labor—could create the most powerful country on Earth. He was right, but that vision required both a massive expansion of government as well as the wholesale violation of property rights. It also required overlooking the moral outrage of slavery, which was an economic asset that the federal government was not yet willing to question.

Railroads require a huge amount of land, and to build a national system, the government had to seize and redistribute an area equivalent to the entire state of South Carolina. The land was seized under the principle of eminent domain, which holds that the government can force the sale of private property if it is overwhelmingly in the public interest. Two irreconcilable forms of freedom were at stake:

a nation's freedom to maximize its own prosperity, and an individual's freedom to own and control land. Prosperity won. In the words of an 1837 court case named *Bloodgood v. Mohawk*, it was the railroad's ability to "annihilate distance" that made it indispensable to the public good and therefore unstoppable in court.

The building of America's railroads was the largest and most ambitious public works project of the industrial era and consumed men almost as fast as it did steel and timber. Railroad work relied on high explosives to blow holes through inconvenient geography and was so dangerous that slave owners often refused to contract out their slaves because they didn't want to lose them. Workers throughout the rest of the country—and much of the South—were often Irish and Chinese immigrants who arrived in America so poor that railroad companies felt free to essentially work them to death. Roughly 1,200 men died working on the Transcontinental Railroad, for example, though the exact number is not known because employers didn't even bother keeping careful records.

Like warfare, building a railroad is crushingly monotonous when it isn't absolutely deadly. First, surveyors staked out routes that made huge detours around anything they couldn't blast through. Timber fallers then cleared first-growth forest with axes and crosscut saws and blew massive stumps out of the ground with dynamite. Only then could an army of laborers start leveling the trackbed. When the laborers were done, crossties and rails were laid out on top ballast and the whole thing was pinned down by "spikers" who counted three strokes to the spike, ten spikes to the rail, and four hundred rails to the mile.

A good crew could lay a mile of track a day except in the mountains, where thousands of men could be stalled in the same place for months. Prostitutes, con men, gamblers, and murderers poured into these work camps as soon as they were established. "The frontier was the principal area of single male brutality," observes historian David Courtwright, who has studied violence in all-male groups. "The surplus of young men, widespread bachelorhood, sensitivity about honor, racial hostility, heavy drinking, religious indifference, group indulgence in vice, ubiquitous armament and inadequate law enforcement were concentrated on the frontier."

Railroad towns and other male-dominated communities had mortality rates that rivaled battlefields, and that did not change until women began to migrate westward and have children. The railroad town of Laramie, Wyoming, had so many murders that the town undertaker often just carted the bodies into the desert and dumped them. Benton, Wyoming, lost 7 percent of its population to murder in the first two months of its existence. As dangerous as railroad work was, a Union Pacific employee was four times more likely to die after hours in towns like Benton and Laramie than on the job itself.

The dangers didn't end after the railroads were built. Early steam engines were considered so risky that the president of the Erie Railroad insisted on doing the inaugural run entirely alone in case there was an accident. Railroad technology was brand new, and there were dangers associated with it that no engineer or actuary could possibly think up. Who could have imagined a swarm of grasshoppers so thick that their crushed bodies could derail trains in Pennsylvania in 1836? How could a twenty-three-year-old railroad worker named Edgar Herenden have known that a "frog"—a mechanical track switch—would grab his foot and not let go until a train ran over him in 1873? And when O. M. Wilmot leaned out the window of his locomotive while driving over a Vermont bridge in 1894, why would he worry about clearances that were so tight, a post would take his head off?

Workers usually died individually, but passengers often died by the trainload. Eighty-nine people lost their lives when an iron trestle failed in its entirety—a so-called square fall—and dropped a whole train into a gorge near Ashtabula, Ohio, in 1876. Many people who survived the fall died in fires that were ignited by lanterns and coal stoves in the wreckage. Eighty-eight people drowned in their compartments when a trestle failed and shunted their train into a flooded creek outside Eden, Colorado, in 1904. These tragedies could have been prevented by better track maintenance. Harder to guard against were the complex interactions of trains, signals, and bad timing. In 1905, a mile-long freight train—moving only six miles an hour—braked to avoid a collision in the Harrisburg yards and pitched some of its boxcars onto another track. Unfortunately, one of those cars was packed with dynamite, which was detonated by a passenger train that just happened to pass at that moment. Twenty-three people were killed and more than one hundred injured. Some of the older survivors must have thought they were back on the battlefields of Antietam and Gettysburg.

Industrial carnage was new to society and civilians were not prepared for it. In fact, the first medical diagnosis for psychological trauma was called "railroad spine," because it was so closely associated with the mass casualties of railroad accidents. In 1903, the Duquesne Limited was running at sixty miles an hour outside Connellsville, Pennsylvania, when she hit a load of timber that had fallen off the freight train that preceded her. It was nighttime and the timber was strewn along a curve, so the engineer had no chance to throw the brakes.

The baggage car derailed and was hurled into the Youghiogheny River. The smoking car, packed with men who had come forward from the passenger cars, flipped and landed on the engine. The impact cracked the boiler, which was pressurized to three hundred pounds per square inch, and escaping steam "cooked the passengers alive." Since very few women smoked, they were mostly in Pullman cars at the rear and could hear their husbands screaming as they died. The force of the collision demolished the engine, ripped almost every car off its trucks, threw a seven-thousand-gallon water tank entirely over the train, and killed seventy-eight people.

The tracks had all the dangers of heavy industry but also ran smack through nature. The trains were so heavy and loud, though, that it was easy for us to forget they weren't the only danger out there. In central Pennsylvania we got caught in a summer thunderstorm that soaked us immediately and sent runoff boiling out of culverts and sheeting down hillsides. It was almost dark and there was nowhere to sleep that wasn't badly angled or completely underwater. One of the men finally looked at me and said, "You know that I must really want to be out here because I have *way* better options than this."

We'd all been in a certain amount of combat and there was something about our endeavor—the simplicity, the hardship, the proximity of death—that reminded us of those days. Most of the trip was done in segments over the course of a year. Halfway through, one man dropped out and others later filled in; one section was just two of us. We called our trip "the Last Patrol," and it seemed like a long hard weird thing to do until we were actually out there, when suddenly it was so obvious that we rarely even caught ourselves wondering why we were doing it. The things that had to happen out there were so clear and simple—eat, walk, hide, sleep—that just getting through the day felt like scripture: a true and honest accounting of everything that underlies the frantic performance of life.

The night of the downpour we slept under a hardware-store tarp in a patch of skunkweed near the river, and I stayed awake listening to the wind in case it ramped up to that high shriek that means treetops are going to start snapping. I'd decided that if that happened, we would wade into the current and sit out the storm on a little brush-covered island I'd spotted. No falling trees could reach us there, and I doubted the river would rise beyond what we could handle.

In the morning the river was at our toes and the island was gone. If we'd gone out there, we'd probably be dead. That was scripture. That was the world letting you know where you stood.

The temptation to ignore reality while believing in a

divine benevolence that will protect you from harm has gotten a lot of people killed over the ages. What truly *is* benevolent, though—what will save you over and over, or often die trying—are other people. In 1996, a southbound MARC commuter train with 150 passengers ran a signal outside Silver Spring, Maryland, and wound up on a collision course with a northbound Amtrak headed for Chicago. The MARC had her engine in the rear, which meant that the lead passenger car would absorb most of the impact. The engineer had roughly fifteen seconds. He threw the brake and ran forward through his train shouting warnings to the passengers. The 130-ton Amtrak engine ripped the lead MARC car in half lengthwise and set the whole thing on fire with spilled diesel. All three crew members died trying to save people in the lead car, and all but eight passengers made it out alive.

The engineer's reaction was not one that could be taught or drilled into him; it was almost certainly instinctive. The willingness to risk death for non-kin is unique to humans and may serve to keep large groups from splitting into smaller ones that would have an even harder time defending themselves. The word *freedom* comes from *vridom*, which means "beloved" in medieval German, and is thought to reflect the idea that only people in one's immediate group were considered worthy of having rights or protection. Outsiders, on the other hand, could be tortured, enslaved, or killed at will. This was true throughout the world and for most of human history, and neither law nor religion nor common decency held otherwise.

The corollary was that if the enemy was not going to show mercy, you might as well fight to the death. Freedom as a supreme value was born of the fact that there were really no alternatives worth considering, and the result was that the freest people were often the most warlike. Nearly a thousand Sicarii Jews committed mass suicide in their besieged city of Masada in 73 BCE, for example, when it became clear that Roman soldiers would eventually breach the walls and enslave everyone they didn't kill. According to Roman accounts, each Sicarii man supposedly killed his own family and then drew straws to kill one another until the last man killed himself. The Romans entered a city that was entirely inhabited by the dead.

The genetic consequences of surrender or defeat could be catastrophic. Around five thousand years ago, nomadic steppe horsemen known as the Yamnaya migrated across Europe and invaded the Iberian Peninsula. They were an exceedingly aggressive, hierarchical people who traveled in all-male groups and fought with axes from the backs of horse-drawn chariots. The Iberians had probably never even seen a horse before, much less ridden one. Over the course of several generations the Yamnaya either killed or somehow out-bred the entire male population of Iberia but spared the lives of the young women, whose DNA—along with that of their conquerors—can still be found in the modern population of Spain. The men failed to repel the invaders and were entirely scrubbed from the human gene pool.

Granting rights to the vanquished was a radical idea that did not establish itself in Western thought until the mid-seventeenth century, when a Dutch scholar named Hugo Grotius began his attempt to regulate warfare by observing that men must "not believe that *nothing* is allowable, or that everything is." It could be said that the idea of personal freedom as a legal right to be extended by the powerful to the weak got its start with Grotius and his attempts to codify the laws of war. If soldiers had rights during war then surely civilians did during peace, and the power of the monarchy could finally start to be disputed.

Grotius based his ideas on something called natural law, which held that human beings—because they were created by God—had rights, such as liberty, that could not be taken away. To do so would be to subvert God's will. Natural law was easy to circumvent, though, because a government or army could just consider the enemy to be subhuman, which happens naturally enough in war anyway. Christian and Muslim societies around the world clearly viewed themselves as superior to other faiths, and many tribal societies refer to themselves as "The People," or "The Real People," generally classifying everyone else as barbarians, animals, or worse. The ancient Greek word for slave—*andrapodon*—was derived from the word for cattle and essentially meant "animal with human feet." Once you have dehumanized others to that degree, you don't have to worry about killing or enslaving God's children, because God's *real* children are supposedly limited to you and your tribe or clan.

There are long-standing evolutionary origins for this bias. Our closest primate relatives, chimpanzees, occasionally kill a member of their own troop but rarely commit desecrations upon the body. When groups of males ambush and kill males of a rival troop, however, they often tear the victim's body to pieces, drinking his blood and tearing off strips of his flesh. According to primatologist Jane Goodall, they "dechimpize" him by treating him like prey. Once the invading chimps have killed off all their male rivals, they mate with the females and incorporate them into their troop—much like the Yamnaya did in Iberia.

It was not until the sweeping human rights laws of the twentieth century that freedom stopped being a question of fighting off one's enemies. International treaties established mechanisms for imposing sanctions or even taking military action against regimes that committed gross human rights violations, and that made freedom a concern of virtually the entire world. Enshrining human rights as the apex of international law is one of the greatest achievements of Western society—perhaps greater than landing on the moon or decoding the human genome—but depends entirely on maintaining a delicate balance between national sovereignty and collective action. All it takes to destroy that balance is for one powerful nation—Hitler's Germany, for example— to decide they're better off doing whatever they want and suffering the consequences than abiding by the treaties. In the case of Germany, it almost worked.

In 1604, the Ottoman Empire decided that the small, mountainous principality of Montenegro had to be crushed. The Montenegrins were a famously warlike people who had always rejected any form of dominion and supposedly feared nothing except dying peacefully in bed. They inhabited a land that was too poor to support concentrations of people larger than a village, but these communities came together immediately when they were invaded. The men always kept a wool blanket over their shoulder to sleep in if need be and dressed in a long cassock that was sashed around the waist and jammed full of weapons. They never went to war with anything less than a pistol, a musket, and a sword.

The Ottoman invasion of Montenegro was a classic example of how a large army can be routed by a handful of determined locals. The Ottomans boasted twelve thousand men, including cavalry and artillery, and faced a mere nine hundred Montenegrins. The Montenegrins were unfazed and sent three-man raiding parties out all night long before attacking at dawn, killing a third of the Ottoman army before the rest fled. The Ottomans invaded Montenegro several times over the next decade, each time more or less doubling the size of their army without ever achieving a lasting victory. "After a major military defeat the tribesmen simply operated in small guerilla bands," observes anthropologist Christopher Boehm of Montenegrin defensive strategy. "By burning crops and hiding away livestock and by cutting off the enemy supply lines, they made certain that their rugged natural fortress could not be occupied permanently, except at an exorbitantly high cost. . . . The Montenegrins lived a locally autonomous life while their neighbors remained in bondage."

Across a broad range of species—chimpanzees, walruses, lions, elk, mice—larger males and groups of males invariably win physical confrontations with each other, but that is not the case with humans. It is a quality entirely unique to humans that a smaller entity, like the Montenegrins, could defeat a larger one. Were this not so, freedom would effectively be impossible: Every group would be run by a single large male, and the world would be dominated by fascist mega-states, like the Ottomans, that could easily crush insubordinate populations. But that's not what the world looks like. Large armies—or people—are stronger than small ones but usually slower and less efficient. This is true at every scale, from open warfare to street corner fistfights. Because the outcome of any human conflict cannot be predicted with certainty, the powerful often end up having to negotiate with the weak, and those negotiations invariably revolve around freedom.

Human violence reaches way back into our evolutionary past and is usually about the same things that are important to chimps: resources, territory, and sexual access to females. Because successful aggression rewards males with all of those things, they tend to have more offspring than low-status males, and the genetics of aggression become even more deeply encoded in the gene pool. (Unlike chimps, bonobo groups are dominated by female alliances that are able to flourish in an environment that is blessed with plenty of food and no competition from mountain gorillas.) Among chimps, fights with outsiders are lopsided ambushes that often result in death, but conflicts between males of the same troop are more balanced. Dominant male chimps bully almost everyone, and when they attempt to bully each other, the larger and stronger male almost always forces the other to submit. That avoids all-out fights that could leave both combatants injured.

Humans are exquisitely attuned to dominance for presumably the same reason. Body language and facial expressions underlay a host of social interactions and are very effective at communicating important information about a person, particularly social rank. By assessing "competency," people can predict, with almost 70 percent accuracy, winners of U.S. Senate races based on a one-second glimpse of the candidates' faces as they campaign. People can accurately assess dominant and submissive traits in others by seeing photographs of them for only 4/100ths of a second—so-called thin-slice judgments. People who have no idea how to play basketball can detect which team is winning or losing by noticing unconscious dominant and submissive behaviors in the players during brief video clips.

Men who score high on the dominance scale generally maintain a wide stance around others, square their shoulders, puff out their chest, hold their chin up, and generally take up as much room as possible. Submissive men do the opposite. Dominant men have significantly higher testosterone levels than nondominant men, and much lower levels of the stress hormone cortisol—both of which are associated with disease resistance and leadership. Testosterone is correlated so strongly with both aggression and wide facial structures in men that it's possible to predict roughly how much time a hockey player will spend in the penalty box during a season by measuring the width of his face. Winning a fight or athletic competition further boosts testosterone levels, which in turn make the dominant man more likely to win the next fight or competition.

Unconscious submission is devastating to a person's chances of winning a fight. In pre-match publicity, boxers who allow themselves a small smile—a classic appeasement cue—are statistically less likely to win the fight than men who only frown. Such signals are known as "leakage" in the world of professional fighting. "It's a sort of involuntary communication—it's deference, it's appeasement," says a former fighter and competitive weightlifter named Justin "Master Chim" Garcia, who trains people out of an old plumbing-supply warehouse in the Bronx, New York. "We want a [fighting] culture that strongly opposes leakage. The only time to communicate weakness is to manipulate. Only the weak mind adds suffering to circumstance."

In addition to masking fear, a smaller fighter must keep his mind calm, his eyes open, and his heart rate steady—think, look, and breathe. "What we've found is that endurance is the most important thing," says Chael Sonnen, a former wrestler and fighter who competed at 220 pounds. "You want to fight the guy one weight class above you, because that's not enough to matter, but over the course of a fight, he's simply going to get tired faster. If you have an adversary that's larger than you, you automatically default into quickness, finesse, and endurance."

As a result, human size and strength are not great predictors of who is going to win a fight. Street fights are hard to study because they happen so randomly, but all of the fighting sports—boxing, karate, wrestling, grappling—are reasonable proxies for actual violence. In mixed martial arts, which integrates all forms of fighting into something that is probably very close to primordial combat, smaller fighters win about half the time against larger ones. Pre-reservation Apache believed that there was special "wrestling power" that could easily make up for small stature. "A man . . . can throw a man twice his size if he uses the power on him," an Apache warrior told anthropologist Grenville Goodwin in the 1930s. "He does not do it by his strength at all, but by his power. There is no name for this power at all except that known to the man who has it."

The reason size and strength do not absolutely determine outcome is that tactics play a huge role in human conflict. The central conundrum of fighting is that you cannot dominate your opponent without attacking him, but attacking ruins your defense and opens you up to counterattack. (One classic defensive position comes from our most basic instincts: hands up to protect the face, chin down to protect the throat, and arms in close to guard the torso. A child who is being tickled will naturally adopt an almost identical pose.) In addition to leaving you momentarily vulnerable, attacking uses up a lot of energy. One good punch can end a fight, but that punch can be slipped by something as subtle and efficient as the tilt of a head. Ten good punches in a row will leave even a trained fighter gasping for breath, while slipping them costs the other combatant almost nothing.

When Manny Pacquiao fought Floyd Mayweather Jr. in a highly anticipated fight in Las Vegas in 2015, Pacquiao maintained a ferocious offense until halfway through the sixth round, when he forced Mayweather against the ropes. Pacquiao unleashed sixteen punches in a row, almost completely unopposed, with Mayweather blocking some, slipping others, and eating the rest. That seems to have been the turning point; eventually Pacquiao simply ran out of gas and took a step back, releasing Mayweather from the ropes. You can't hear it, but you can see it: Mayweather shaking his head and mouthing the word *nope*, before starting his counterattack. Mayweather dominated the next six rounds and won the fight by unanimous decision.

Mayweather and Pacquiao were the same size; the fight seemed to tip on the disproportionate energy costs of an offense compared to a defense. When it comes to a matchup between a smaller fighter and a larger one, each has a particular advantage. Large fighters are usually stronger and can outmuscle opponents if they get their hands on them. And small fighters have less mass to set into motion, so they can move faster and use less energy doing it. If fights were held in elevators or shower stalls that wouldn't help much, but they're not; even a sixteen-by-sixteen-foot boxing ring can seem like acres of canvas with a fighter who really knows how to move.

Large, aggressive men also tend to attack first, but if they don't win quickly, they may not win at all. Strength does not increase linearly with body weight: the world record for the deadlift in the 148-pound weight class is just shy of 700 pounds, whereas the world record for the 308-pound weight class is 939 pounds. Doubling the weight class does not double how much a man can deadlift, in other words; it only increases the amount by about 25 percent. That is a dangerous tradeoff because large muscles require more oxygen to function, and if you are working so hard that you cannot replace that oxygen fast enough, you will go into oxygen debt. Your vision will blur, your movements will slow, and eventually you won't be able to stand up. At the same level of activity, all of that will happen to a large person before a small one.

In 1969, at the height of his powers, boxer Muhammad Ali was placed in front of a balsa-wood board and told to smash it with one of his deadly jabs when a light flashed.

His brain required only 15/100ths of a second to process the signal—much faster than the proverbial blink of an eye—but his fist was even faster. It snapped out and hit the board in 4/100ths of a second. Ali could also deliver a devastating six-punch combination—two jabs, a hook, a right to the body, another hook, and then a right to the head—in just over two seconds. If he was anything like some of the other top boxers who have been tested, his most powerful punches probably hit with as much as one thousand pounds of force.

It took three times as long for Ali's brain to process the flashing light than for his fist to react, which means that in a fight, his fist would easily hit his opponent's face before his opponent had a chance to move it. Neurologically, that should mean there's no way to slip a punch, which would turn fights into contests of pure punching power, but that's not what happens. The brain may be slow but it's incredibly perceptive, and the body may be fast but it's incredibly revealing. Long before the fist actually starts moving, the puncher's face and body emit a cascade of signals that reveal what is about to happen. Those signals are decoded by the opponent and used to begin slipping punches that haven't even happened yet.

To pick up these cues, it helps to keep a kind of broad, general focus rather than fixating on your opponent's fists. The perceptive power of the brain in this undirected mode is so strong that it seems to border on a kind of telepathy. Test subjects can tell winning poker hands, for example, by watching two-second clips of professional players moving their chips to the center of the table to place a bet. Players with winning hands were almost imperceptibly smoother and looser in their body movements. (Their faces were unobservable in the study. A separate study found that facial expression—which is easy to mask—did not help observers judge the strength of a hand at all.) And the same is true of athletes: If you show basketball players a brief video of fellow players taking a free throw, roughly two-thirds of the time they can determine whether or not he will make the shot, based solely on the movement of the arm. There is something about grace that tells athletes what is about to happen.

In short, quicker, more efficient movement gives small fighters an advantage over large ones, and unconscious perceptions allow them to see punches before they have been launched. Were either not true, large fighters would regularly crush small ones, but they don't. This allows humans to confront or disobey the largest male in the group, which is a departure from millions of years of primate evolution. In addition, the invention of weapons served to greatly equalize size differences between combatants. "The possession by all men . . . of the means to kill secretly anyone perceived as a threat to their own well-being not only limits predation and exploitation, it also serves as a powerful leveling mechanism," observes anthropologist James Woodburn about the nomadic Hadza of East Africa. "Inequalities of wealth, power and prestige are potential sources of envy and resentment and can be dangerous for the holders."

And the basic dynamics of asymmetric conflict readily scale up. Insurgents like the Montenegrins cannot hope to beat a large conventional military in open combat, so they don't even try. Instead, they do what small athletes do: they stay mobile, they avoid standing toe-to-toe and trading blows, and they strike only when they can get away. Conventional armies burn through more fuel, munitions, and food in the same way that large fighters burn through more oxygen, and even wealthy nations can't afford to maintain that level of effort indefinitely. The logistical demands of a modern, mechanized army are so enormous that most of its resources go into simply sustaining itself; no more than one-third of its soldiers are directly engaged in combat, and usually far less. Insurgents, on the other hand, are almost all engaged in combat—often including senior commanders. And they never have to win; they just have to keep not losing.

Airpower is also of limited value against smaller forces. In fact, there is almost an inversion of ordinary military principles: The fewer enemy there are, the harder they are to kill and less likely they are to be defeated. A million-man army can probably be destroyed faster than a thousand-man insurgency because it's completely dependent on command hierarchy and resupply; destroy those things and there is no army. Most insurgencies, on the other hand, are composed of semiautonomous cells that are dependent on the society they live in, and targeting civilians is a war crime. It also turns the populace against the invaders and drives them into the arms of the insurgents. Bombers and attack aircraft can drop devastating munitions on the battlefield, but they are easy for insurgents to avoid and incredibly costly to operate. There does not seem to be enough jet fuel in the world to keep enough aircraft aloft to kill all the people who are willing to die fighting them. Airpower alone has never broken an insurgency, and reliance on it could almost be considered a sign of strategic failure.

On the ground, combat soldiers in the U.S. military carry loads of up to 140 pounds on approach marches and seventy or eighty pounds in combat, including a thirty-pound ballistic vest that traps heat and sends body temperature soaring. Machine gunners and ammo bearers routinely carry a lot more than that. The weight is a problem in hot weather, when soldiers require as much as two or three gallons of water a day to avoid dehydration and heat stroke. According to the Asymmetric Warfare Group (AWG), an elite high-mobility unit within the U.S. military, soldiers are often reduced to maneuver speeds of one or two miles an hour by such loads, and yet they are fighting insurgents who can move several times as fast.

The result is that Western troops struggle to corner and defeat even lightly armed insurgents. The parallel between current-day Taliban forces in Afghanistan and the Apache of the 1860s and '70s is so obvious that the School of Advanced Military Studies at Fort Leavenworth, Kansas, has published a monograph on the Indian Wars. "The failed subjugation attempts assisted the Apache to develop a warrior culture based on resistance and survival through tactical action," notes the author, Major Stephen P. Snyder, a former AWG commander. (The AWG was disbanded in 2020.) "The Apache . . . created a warrior that was an expert at fighting in austere environments, understood the use of irregular tactics to render a numerically superior force vulnerable, and possessed an intrinsic warrior ideology that defeated all previous foreign invaders."

After two decades of war in Afghanistan, the United States found itself having to negotiate with an insurgency that lacked airpower, tanks, heavy artillery, and sometimes even boots. A relatively small number of Taliban insurgents fought the most powerful military in the world to a standstill, and a prior generation of Afghans did the same thing to the former Soviet Union. The Taliban represent an oppressive ideology that has almost no respect for human rights, but many insurgencies *are* fighting for those rights. And if all insurgencies and uprisings were easily crushed, there would be no possibility for political change—or freedom—in the world. Among other outcomes, the United States would not exist.

However it is defined, freedom is due, in part, to the fact that powerful nations do not always win wars and powerful men do not always win fights. In fact, as often as not, they lose.

BOOK THREE · THINK

We passed Tyrone in a thumping rain, skirting a maintenance yard that forced us into some overgrown bottomland along the river. There was a deer-hunting blind not a quarter mile from downtown and then a span over the river that we crossed at a low trot, hoping the workers wouldn't see us. Moving at our long-distance pace now, countryside reeling past: a tiny cemetery filled with dead Germans and a quiet little town that took no notice of us and a stretch of open parkland with a little creek running through it where we could fill our bottles.

A freight went by pulling scores of Karo corn syrup tanks. We moved until a steady rain settled in and then we strung up a tarp in the galloping darkness. I took the machete and chopped slabs of bark off a dead locust and made a pyramid over a bundle of pine twigs and dead grass that I managed to light after a couple of tries. I split small sticks lengthwise and laid them dryside in and then did the same with larger sticks and when the fire was hot enough to burn anything, I piled on all the wood I had. We put a pot of riverwater to boil for spaghetti and settled back with our cigarettes and our water bottles and our sore legs stretched out before us. After dinner we went to sleep in a row with the dog lying beside me and the fire spitting behind us as it died in the rain. One of God's great oversights is that dogs don't live as long as men, I thought. And that men don't move as fast as dogs.

A front came through before sunup and now towering cumulous clouds dragged their great shadows across the land. We didn't bother with breakfast and moved on Altoona fast, hoping to eat in seats at a table, but we passed downtown unable to find a diner or even people. A boarded-up hotdog joint with "ESTABLISHED IN 1918" painted on the windows and the long empty Altoona rail yards, once the largest locomotive factory in the world. Downtown we finally spotted a clutch of people smoking under an awning, most on walkers and one in a wheelchair. While we stood there another man walked up and asked us how to hop a freight train. He was black in a completely white town and looked cold and tired and alone. He said he'd left his girl in Pittsburgh and had some kind of job waiting for him in Atlantic City but got stranded in Altoona. He was living outside but eating at a soup kitchen once a day and didn't have enough money to move on. "Most of the people at the soup kitchen *live* here," he said. "They ain't even homeless. That's how bad this place is."

I told him we didn't know anything about hopping

freights and had a dog with us anyway, but if he walked twenty miles a day he'd be in Atlantic City in a couple of weeks. I wished him luck and we angled out of town to a place where we could get back onto the tracks without anyone noticing. We passed a pair of dark Gothic houses with fieldstone foundations and wide porches, heavily columned, that looked built to withstand centuries of small-town American life. Each was now the local headquarters of one of the country's two political parties, flags leveled at each other and placards arrayed across twenty feet of bad macadam.

The tracks circled town and then ran west up Burgoon Run, which came out of a series of reservoirs tucked into Mount Logan. We were off the Juniata for good now and on the edge of the great Allegheny escarpment, crossing into the Conemaugh drainage that flowed west to the Kiskiminetas River and the Allegheny and the Ohio. Steam engines geared to huge windlasses used to hoist canalboats and trains from the Juniata up the Allegheny Front, then release them into the Conemaugh watershed for the downhill trip to Pittsburgh. The hauling was done on three-and-a-half-inch hemp, and passengers would get out and walk in case the line parted and the whole works went back down the mountain.

The tracks clung to the slope above Burgoon and crossed creeks on massive quarrystone trestles. At Scotch Gap the tracks followed the contours upstream and ran deep into

Mount Logan before crossing. The stoneworks were fifty feet high and Scotch Gap Run flowed through them in a huge oval culvert, the pretty Pennsylvania countryside pasted on the other side like a travel poster. We made camp below the stonework so that the freight trains groaned and shrieked into the turn directly above our heads and it was impossible not to calculate the distance a boxcar car might travel if it somehow came airborne on that curve. Everything trains do they do big. In 2013, a trainload of Bakken Formation crude derailed in Lac-Mégantic, Canada, and set off an explosion that leveled the entire downtown and killed forty-two people. Another five were never accounted for.

There was an old campfire and beer cans and a scatter of brass in the leaves, which made sense because a jeep track came down the mountain from the direction of town and people liked the spot for the same reasons we did: lots of water and no one could see you and deadwood everywhere, you didn't even need an ax. You could shoot at passing boxcars all day long and no one would know. I had no desire to make some kind of last stand against the locals so I kept the things I needed most next to my head when I slept; that way we could just grab our stuff and go. I wore my headlamp around my neck so I'd never have to look for it. I kept a knife in my boots, which were loosely laced so I could just drop my feet into them and run. My pillow was a rolled-up jacket.

I had a lighter and maps in my pocket and a water jug next to my boots. The machete was in a tree trunk. The dog was at our feet. It wasn't a lot, but you could keep yourself warm and dry for a while with that.

The rest of our gear was so easily replaced that it wasn't worth having a fight over or even a bad conversation. A tarp and metal pot and a hundred feet of parachute cord we could get at a hardware store for fifty bucks. A machete or short-handled ax for the woods and a small stove that runs on white gas for the city. A medium-grit stone. A pump filter for water. A big metal stir spoon. Needle and thread. Toenail clippers. We carried oatmeal and coffee and brown sugar to eat in the morning and cheese and flour tortillas and pasta and tomato paste for everything else. A bottle of hot sauce and a flask of olive oil and a few onions. We bought food every few days so that we could go faster. If you can't run a mile with all your gear, you've got too much gear.

We built up the fire in the morning and cooked coffee and oatmeal and then climbed up to the grade and stepped out toward Horseshoe Curve and Sugar Run and Gallitzin on the other side of Tunnel Hill. Horseshoe was a 220-degree curve that contoured around a valley instead of crossing directly over a steep gorge called Glenwhite Run. Engineers coming out of Horseshoe can briefly see the back of their train ahead of them. Horseshoe Curve was such a feat of engineering—and so crucial to eastbound freight—that it was on Hitler's target list for bombing and sabotage because it would have been so time-consuming to rebuild.

There are still arrest orders for anyone on the tracks at Horseshoe. There is a gazebo and visitor center at the crux of the curve, and a group of Mennonites were gathered at some picnic tables waiting for trains to go by when we showed up, the women in bonnets and the men well dressed and stern. They stared as we trudged past, except the young boys, who pointed excitedly and shouted. A mile farther we stopped at an abandoned switching house to drink some water and smoke a cigarette. Nearby was an old steel communications box with a whip antenna and voices coming from the inside. We gathered around and listened to ten minutes of Conrail radio traffic before shouldering our packs and moving on. There was no mention of men at Horseshoe so we moved without worry.

The tracks bent west up Sugar Run, and the rest of the day we walked into the sun toward the triple boreholes of Tunnel Hill. It's a tough little neighborhood built atop tailings and mining rubble a few miles from what is known as the Eastern Continental Divide. Water that falls on the east side of the divide runs back to the Atlantic, and water that falls on the west side runs to the Mississippi. West, west, the rest of my country lay.

. . .

The central problem for human freedom is that groups that are well organized enough to defend themselves against others are well organized enough to oppress their own. Power is so readily abused that one could almost say that its concentration is antithetical to freedom. Democracy—both in its modern form and in its original, indigenous form—is an attempt to balance the two. The Iroquois Great Law of Peace, for example, was established generations before whites arrived in North America and served as a philosophical starting point for the U.S. Constitution. In both Western and Native traditions, a warrior culture was fostered that could defend the tribe or nation but was under the direct control of civilians. And civilians had to be willing to give up leadership when they were overruled by a majority, because they presumably valued having no power in a fair system more than they valued having all the power in an unfair one.

The great virtue of hunter-gatherer societies around the world was that, although leaders understandably had more prestige than other people, they didn't have more *rights*. Unlike European monarchs, they could not leverage their power to gain access to wealth and resources, and they could not skirt the rules and laws that governed everybody else.

Christianity was a high moral system based on the preaching of a destitute ascetic, but it somehow became the dominant faith of a medieval society where kings could commit murder without consequences and the powerful could rape, steal, and plunder even among their own. (As late as 1936, a Spanish aristocrat named Gonzalo de Aguilera y Munro lined up the laborers on his estate outside Salamanca and executed six of them at random to discourage the rest from demanding better working conditions. Not only was he never charged with the crime, he boasted about it publicly under the new fascist regime in Spain.) Far from acting as an impediment to abuse, the Church was often allied with aristocrats like Aguilera, participating in military campaigns during the Middle Ages and even torturing and killing perceived enemies. The only advocate for the poor seemed to be Jesus, but century after century, the poor just seemed to stay poor.

At the very least, this bizarre system required a kind of martial fortitude on the part of the powerful. Kings were expected to lead their armies in person, which put them in the midst of a kind of hacking slaughter that clearly spared no one. That could qualify as a kind of rough egalitarianism, but the last European monarch to die in combat was King James IV of Scotland, who invaded England in 1513 with thirty thousand soldiers, noblemen, and clergy. He saw a third of his force annihilated before he himself was cut down. Almost thirty years earlier, King Richard III of England had been unhorsed and killed at Bosworth Field. After those battles, the kingly virtue of fighting alongside noblemen and commoners began to die out, and monarchs were content to order other men to do their fighting and dying for them.

There is obviously little merit in having leaders of modern democracies do the work of combat infantry—even lieutenant colonels don't do that unless absolutely necessary—but that doesn't mean sacrifice need disappear from public life. In a deeply free society, not only would leaders be barred from exploiting their position, they would also be expected to make the same sacrifices and accept the same punishments as everyone else. The authors of the American Constitution were among the wealthiest and most powerful men of their society and yet, with a few narrow exceptions, they made themselves subject to the same laws and penalties that governed others. (Many also risked being hanged for treason if the British won the war.) It was one of the few times in recorded history that a society's elite stripped themselves of special protections and offered to serve the populace, rather than demanding to be served by them.

Although democracy may not survive as a broad form of

freedom, its core virtue of insisting leaders be accountable to others and willing to make sacrifices is crucial to any group that faces adversity. In that, democracy has essentially reproduced hunter-gatherer society, where rigid constraints are put on leaders because self-serving leaders can literally get people killed. But in any society, leaders who aren't willing to make sacrifices aren't leaders, they're opportunists, and opportunists rarely have the common good in mind. They're easy to spot, though: opportunists lie reflexively, blame others for failures, and are unapologetic cowards. Wealthy nations might survive that kind of leadership, but insurgencies and uprisings probably won't; their margins simply aren't big enough. A prerequisite for any such group would seem to be leaders that—like their followers—are prepared to die for the cause.

Hunter-gatherers are generally spared opportunistic leadership because the gap between rich and poor is so narrow—not surprising in economies that don't use currency or stockpile food. As soon as food can be monopolized, though, hunter-gatherers become just as unfair and stratified as everyone else. Archaeological evidence from across the Pacific Northwest indicates that some Native communities figured out how to restrict access to riverine salmon fisheries and quickly instituted a powerful elite that built large houses, kept slaves, and passed wealth from generation to generation. But most Native peoples lived off the land in a way that could not be monopolized. A survey of several hundred tribes native to North America found that nearly 90 percent of the ones with no large food surpluses also had no political inequality. Conversely, social stratification was found in almost 90 percent of tribes that *did* stockpile food or monopolize its production.

And even at the subsistence level, hunter-gatherers often go to great lengths to make sure skilled hunters are not held in overly high esteem. It's not that they are against excellence—in fact they depend on it—but they know how badly pride and ego can destabilize a group. "A Hadza returning to camp having shot a large animal is expected to exercise restraint," observed anthropologist James Woodburn. "He sits down quietly with the other men and allows the blood on his arrow shaft to speak for him."

The distribution of income in a society is called the "Gini coefficient," named after an Italian sociologist named Corrado Gini, who published a paper on the topic in 1912. A society where one person earns all the money and everyone else earns none, effectively has a Gini coefficient of 1.0; and a society where everyone earns the same amount has a coefficient of zero. Neither is desirable. Moderate differences in income motivate people because they have a reasonable chance of bettering their circumstances, and extreme differences discourage people because their efforts look futile. A study of twenty-one small-scale societies around the world found that hunter-gatherers like the Hadza—who presumably represent the most efficient possible system for survival in a hostile environment—have Gini coefficients as low as .25. In other words, they are far closer to absolute income equality than to absolute monopoly.

Because oppression from one's own leaders is as common a threat as oppression from one's enemies, Gini coefficients are one reliable measure of freedom. Hunter-gatherer societies are not democracies—and many hold women in subordinate family roles—but the relationship between those families and their leaders is almost impervious to exploitation. In that sense they are freer than virtually all modern societies. According to multiple sources, including the Congressional Budget Office, the United States has one of the highest Gini coefficients of the developed world, .42, which puts it at roughly the level of Ancient Rome. (Before taxes, the American Gini coefficient is even higher—almost .6—which is on par with deeply corrupt countries like Haiti, Namibia, and Botswana.) Moreover, the wealth gap between America's richest and poorest families has *doubled* since 1989. Globally, the situation is even more extreme: several dozen extremely rich people control as much wealth as the bottom half of humanity—3.8 billion people.

It's tempting to imagine that economic injustice destabilizes societies to the point where they collapse and have to reform themselves, but the opposite appears to be true. Countries with large income disparities, such as the United States, are among the most powerful and wealthy countries in the world, perhaps because they can protect themselves with robust economies and huge militaries. They're just not very free. Even societies with income disparities that are truly off the chart—medieval Europe had a Gini coefficient of .79—are relatively stable until a cataclysmic event like the plague triggers a radical redistribution of wealth.

During the last decades, progressive reforms have reduced the Gini coefficient—and stabilized the economies—in many Latin American countries. From every standpoint—morally, politically, economically—such reforms are clearly the right thing to do. But throughout the great sweep of human history, egalitarian societies with low Gini coefficients rarely dominate world events. From the Han Dynasty of Ancient China to the Roman Empire to the United States, there seems to be a sweet spot of economic injustice that is moderately unfair to most of its citizens but produces extremely powerful societies. Economist Walter Scheidel calculates that 3,500 years ago, such large-scale states controlled only 1 percent of the Earth's habitable landmass but represented at least *half* the human population. By virtually any metric, that's a successful society. "For thousands of years, most of humanity lived in the shadow of these behemoths," Scheidel writes. "This is the environment that created the 'original one percent,' made up of competing but often closely intertwined elite groups."

The question, then, is, how do ordinary people protect their freedom in the face of such highly centralized state control?

Before dawn on May 8, 1916, an Irish revolutionary named Michael Mallin was led down a flight of stairs into a small courtyard, known as the "Stonebreakers' Yard," at Dublin's infamous Kilmainham Jail. Mallin was forty-one years old, a father of four, and an organizer for the Dublin Silk Weavers' union. But he was also second-in-command of the Irish Citizen Army, which was one of the revolutionary groups that had hoped to overthrow British rule in Ireland. Mallin had been given command of a brigade and told to take over St. Stephen's Green, which he did with a group of men and women armed with everything from bird-hunting guns to Mauser machine pistols. Mallin's forces dug trenches and set up a kitchen and first-aid stations before being driven out by British soldiers shooting down from the surrounding buildings. The combat was intense but would pause for an old man to come and feed the park's ducks every day.

The Easter Rising, as it was known, had at times the odd feeling of street performance or make-believe. Many of the combatants knew each other, and civilians would gather to watch pitched battles as if they were football matches. One brigade went to their positions on the city tram carrying pikes, shotguns, and machine guns like revellers on Halloween. Their commander insisted on paying everyone's fare. Another group was offended when a policeman laughed at the sight of them and accused them of playing soldier.

And then a city hall clerk and theater actor named Sean Connolly shot an unarmed policeman in the head and there was no going back.

The policeman's name was James O'Brien, and he was a longtime veteran of the city police force who was guarding Dublin Castle Gate. A group of armed, uniformed rebels had surprised all of Dublin on Easter morning by massing at the castle gate, and O'Brien raised his arm to stop them from passing. Connolly—who would be dead from a sniper's bullet within hours—raised his rifle and shot O'Brien point-blank. O'Brien stood for a moment and then dropped to the ground, geysering blood from his head. The rebels gaped in amazement at what they had done and then rushed forward.

The rebels were mostly working-class men from Dublin with a smattering of writers and poets among the leaders. There was a women's brigade as well, the Cummann na mBan, and other women scattered throughout the brigades—many of them wives and mothers of men who were fighting. The bullets were often handmade, and the grenades were fashioned from tin cans stuffed with nuts, bolts, and an explosive called gelignite. Many rebels carried Lee-Enfield .303s that had been lifted from British soldiers who spent their nights drinking in the city pubs. Others had old Mauser '71s that kicked so badly, they threw people's shoulders out and spewed three feet of flame out the muzzle. The rebels mustered at half-strength, if that, and knew so little about urban combat that they dispatched someone to Dublin Library to look it up. They hated the English enough to invite the Germans to invade Ireland on their behalf, but the Germans had their hands full on the battlefields of Europe and sent a shipload of weapons instead. The British navy made sure it never reached shore.

The British troops had minimal training as well, and it may be testament to the efficacy of modern weapons that the two sides still achieved such slaughter. Advancing in waves up Northumberland Road, a force of mostly teen-age boys in British uniform ran straight into machine-gun fire from seventeen rebels holed up in buildings around Mount Street Bridge. There were several ways to bypass this bottleneck, but the British command seemed intent on proving a point. British forces eventually took the bridge by simply sending teenagers in faster than the rebels could shoot them, and by the time it was over, more than two hundred English boys lay dead or dying on Northumber-land Road and along the banks of the canal. Many were crumpled in doorways where they had tried to take cover. The rebels lost five men.

Elsewhere in the city looters swarmed through the streets and briefly gave both sides a common enemy. Street children took over a hatter's shop and came out dressed in rags but wearing hunting caps and bowlers. Drunks ran-sacked a waxworks and came out in period costume to do battle on the street with swords and broken bottles. The mayhem did not endear the rebels to the populace, and groups of working-class women—many of whom had sons and husbands in the trenches of France—began to gather in mobs and scream obscenities. Later, after it was all over, many of these same women urged British troops to "bayo-net them" when prisoners were rounded up and marched down the street.

Although the real struggle would come later, an initial British victory was almost inevitable. They had artillery, heavy machine guns, and battle wagons made from old locomotive boilers that carried troops who shot through gunloops. A battleship fired her cannon from the harbor and reinforcements poured in by the day. When the British couldn't get close to the rebels, they shelled them. When they couldn't shell them, they starved them. By the end of the week, the rebels were so exhausted that some had to be carried, asleep, to new positions as they retreated. After six days, the rebels agreed to unconditional surrender and were marched from their positions at gunpoint.

Thousands of rebels and ordinary citizens were detained, and fourteen leaders stood trial for treason. Michael Mallin was one of them. His trial lasted fifteen minutes and was conducted by military personnel who had little if any legal training. There was no jury or stenographer or public witness, and Mallin was allowed no legal counsel. He was found guilty of treason and sentenced to death by firing squad. Given the opportunity to speak, he simply said that he wanted to thank Captain Harry de Courcy-Wheeler, to whom he had surrendered, "for the kindness and consideration that he had shown us during that time."

Mallin was driven from the military barracks, where the trial was held, to Kilmainham Jail, where he would be executed. The route happened to pass his house, and Mallin managed to catch sight of his dog in the yard as he went by. Two nights later, hours before his execution, he wrote a letter to his wife. It was mostly stream of consciousness and seemed seized by regret that he was abandoning her and their children: "My heartstrings are torn to pieces when I think of you and them of our manly James happy go lucky John shy warm Una dady's Girl and oh little Joseph my little man Wife dear Wife I cannot keep the tears back when I think of him he will rest in my arms no more . . . my little man my little man my little man, his name unnerves me again all your dear faces arise before me God bless you God bless you my darlings."

Now the sound of the lockbolt, the groan of the hinges. Now Mallin descending the staircase to the Stonebreakers' Yard. It's barely light and he will never see the sun again, nor his home, nor his family. Mallin is sat on a crate against a stone wall that is already chipped from previous volleys. A piece of paper is pinned to his chest to give the riflemen something to shoot at. A medical examiner will later say that the soldiers were more nervous than the condemned, and that their rifles waved "like a field of corn" when they took aim. Mallin is offered a blindfold, but it is not known if he accepts.

Moments later, he is dead.

. . .

Watching waves of British soldiers run into gunfire on Northumberland Road, it might have occurred to some of the
rebels that there was no reason to expect better treatment
from the British than they gave their own citizens. At that
time, the top 1 percent of British society controlled almost
70 percent of the wealth, and working-class men were being
fed into an industrial war machine across the channel at
rates that were unprecedented in history. At the Battle of
the Somme three months after the Easter Rising, Britain
suffered almost sixty thousand men killed and wounded on
the first day—equivalent to the entire population of County
Wicklow at the time. Like wealth discrepancies, mortality
rates provide a rough indication of relative freedom, and
when social classes die at radically different rates from one
another, some are obviously less free. An important part
of freedom is not having to make sacrifices for people who
don't have to make sacrifices for you.

The failed violence of the Easter Rising turned out to
be a prelude to a much longer fight for independence. At
first the Irish public was furious at the destruction caused
by the rebels, but as stories about the executed men began
to circulate—poet and playwright Thomas MacDonagh was
said to have whistled his way down the prison staircase—the

essential unfairness of the proceedings began to arouse deep disgust. And in their last days, several of the condemned were careful to blame the British government rather than the soldiers themselves, perhaps understanding that working people everywhere were oppressed in similar ways. In another letter to his wife, Mallin said he found "no fault with the soldiers or the police," and urged her to "pray for all the souls who fell in the fight, Irish and English."

The British found that it was easier to kill rebels than to control civilians, and after an initial burst of goodwill, the public turned steadily against them. In the long run, early failure is probably just as great a generator of freedom as early success. To crush the separatist movement, British soldiers arrested too many innocent people, enforced too many harsh laws, and pointed their guns too freely at checkpoints. They were also drunk much of the time. The Easter Rising had managed—or forced—a multitude of rival factions to unite under one political roof, and within two years, the separatist group Sinn Féin won a landslide election. After two years of civil war, England pulled her forces out and granted Ireland complete sovereignty, with an opt-out clause for the Protestant minority in the north. It was a divided land that still faced decades of violence and strife, but the predominantly Catholic districts of Ireland were free of English control for the first time since 1169.

On the face of it, the idea that, given enough time, an impoverished agrarian society could face down a global power fifty miles off their coast seems improbable. In fact, Irish separatists embodied every single trait common to successful insurgencies around the world and, if anything, the long-term odds might have been slightly in their favor. Anyone who wants to overthrow an established power—a government, an army, or even a dominant corporation—must, first and foremost, believe they are fulfilling a kind of historic destiny. People like Michael Mallin need a reason to think their sacrifice was worth it when they hug their children for the last time, and Irish history provides that in spades. Centuries of British rule gave them a clear sense of heroic sacrifice, and the potato famine of the 1840s—which killed or displaced a quarter of the population—turned Ireland into a land of almost mythic suffering. Those attributes were amplified by Irish music and literature during a decades-long cultural awakening that led up to the Easter Rising, and Gaelic was resurrected as a source of national pride in direct defiance of British law.

And many of the insurgents were Catholic, which made independence from Protestant England almost a divine cause. While most people will defend their families without a second thought, dying for an idea usually requires giving ordinary people an extraordinary sense of purpose, and both national suffering and God do that nicely. None of that will help, though, if leaders aren't prepared to make huge sacrifices as well. An insurgency or political movement with leaders who refuse to suffer the same consequences as everyone else is probably doomed. Unfair hierarchies destroy motivation, and motivation is the one thing that underdogs must have more of than everyone else.

Like the American men who signed the Declaration of Independence, Irish separatist leaders must have known that losing to Britain would almost certainly mean their execution for treason. After all, the British still executed their own soldiers for cowardice. What is startling, however, is the level of risk these men tolerated during actual combat. Irish leaders made little distinction between themselves and the soldiers they led; if anything, they sometimes showed a kind of flagrant disregard for their own safety. James Connolly, commander in chief of rebel forces in Dublin, took "no notice of rank," according to one of his men, and insisted on touring frontline positions in person. His main weakness was an almost pathological cheerfulness under fire.

"Heavy firing was taking place, and Connolly insisted on walking out into Abbey Street and giving me instructions as to where I should place a barricade," remembers a seventeen-year-old fighter named Oscar Traynor, who would go on to serve as Ireland's longest-running minister of defense. "Bullets were actually striking the pavement around us. I pointed this out to him and said I thought it was a grave risk . . . and that these instructions could be given inside."

Connolly was wounded twice that week, including by a bullet that destroyed his ankle. As a result, he was the only man who was not able to walk to his own execution. Soldiers carried him into the Stonebreakers' Yard and fired a volley into his chest that also blew out the back of the chair he was tied to.

Women are the final component in defeating a dominant power. First and foremost, they impart a kind of moral legitimacy to protests that could otherwise be dismissed as simple mayhem. And, like small men in a fistfight, they are often underestimated in ways that can be endlessly exploited against an overconfident adversary. During the 1912 mill strike in Lawrence, Massachusetts, for example, immigrant women stood directly in front of National Guard troops and mocked their manhood despite the fact that they had bayonets pointed directly at their bellies. "One policeman can handle ten men," a frustrated city official complained, "while it takes ten policemen to handle one woman."

The Lawrence mill strike occurred during an exceptionally

undemocratic time in America, when thousands of immigrants stopped working to protest living conditions that saw almost one in five infants die before the age of two. Rather than help reform the textile industry, state and federal government cracked down on the protestors. Among other things, they tried to ban midwifery because they were alarmed—as well they might have been—by the idea of women providing crucial skills and services outside of state control. The men who were marching in the street were easily stopped by troops with guns, but the women were almost entirely beyond scrutiny. They established kitchens to feed the strikers, "befriended" soldiers and court officials in order to spy on them, and frisked suspicious men to make sure they weren't scabs. "Women's belief in the public nature of individual misfortune," historian Ardis Cameron has written, "helped women mold grievances into specific targets of protest."

In the end, the strikers won. Immigrant women were effective precisely because they were marginal. Their social networks ran laterally through overpopulated neighborhoods that were almost impossible to infiltrate, and they emphasized the "interconnectedness of individual lives," as Cameron observes, in ways that served to unify disparate groups. Hierarchical male groups are good at mustering on the street and running into gunfire—another important task—but terrible at creating alliances. According to "Big Bill" Haywood, the most notorious of the labor leaders, it was "The women [who] won the strike."

In pitched battles bullets don't distinguish between the sexes, but policemen often do. Rightly or wrongly, society tends to value women's survival more than men's, and that makes machine-gunning them problematic. A British investigation into the loss of the *Titanic* found that men died at much higher rates than women, and that men in first-class cabins had some of the highest mortality rates on the ship—even higher than female crew. If millionaires on sinking ships are willing to give their lifeboat seats to working-class women they don't even know, soldiers are going to balk at opening fire on women on the street. Not that it doesn't happen, but such slaughter is greeted with far more international outrage than the mass killing of men. And commanders who give such orders risk triggering a revolt among their own troops.

In military terminology that makes women a "force multiplier"—a factor that allows soldiers to fight more effectively than another unit of the same size. The lone female separatist who was sentenced to death during the Easter Rising, Constance Markievicz, had her sentence commuted because the British were worried about the political consequences. That can be used in countless ways to flummox even a government that doesn't balk at losing nearly sixty thousand men in a single day.

Seven years after the successful Lawrence strike, steel workers called for a general strike in the mill towns around Pittsburgh. Most of the workers were immigrants from central Europe, and they had a hard time even understanding English, much less taking on the U.S. government. They also had to deal with troopers on horseback who rode right up people's front steps into their houses, and a private security force called the Coal and Iron Police.

A journalist named Mary Heaton Vorse, who had covered the Lawrence strike for *Harper's Weekly* and was now working for a church-sponsored fact-finding mission, traveled by train to Pittsburgh to see if the workers could do it again. (Vorse also covered combat during the First World War and raised three children on a writer's income after her second husband died in 1915.) Vorse had particularly good access to the women in the mill towns, and her account makes it clear that even when they were not protesting in the streets, their work taking care of their families was absolutely crucial to the cause. "The endurance of women was a bulwark of the steel strike," she writes. "Young and burdened down by the cares of their children, the [women] upheld it. There were hundreds of women, and thousands of them scattered through the steel towns who made up their minds that they could hold out a little longer, another week, two weeks more."

The mill workers were striking for fair pay, shorter hours, and less dangerous conditions—some mills averaged a fatality a day. But the strike also went to the heart of fundamental American rights. Pressured by the steel companies, local governments banned all labor meetings and even made it a crime to gather in groups of more than two in public. These local ordinances were so severe that the mayor of Duquesne, Pennsylvania, boasted that "Jesus Christ himself couldn't speak" in his town.

Five thousand men were deputized by the Allegheny County sheriff, a man named Haddock, and given firearms that the steel companies had bought for them. Mounted troops locally known as "Cossacks" were dispatched to the mill towns and began arresting people based on tips from undercover agents who worked for the steel companies. A Senate investigation later found that, among hundreds of transgressions, the police had arrested a woman just for going to the store to get food for her family. They also beat and arrested a man—an American citizen—who was standing in his own doorway, looking. The police seemed to want a level of obedience from people that bordered on servility, and that was precisely the kind of feudal state many of the steelworkers had fled in the first place. The Slovacks, Poles,

Russians, and Hungarians who worked in the steel mills of Pennsylvania may have not realized it, but they were as much standing up for fundamental American rights of free speech and assembly as they were for their own personal interests.

"The strike swept through the country like a flame," wrote Vorse. "Three hundred thousand people thinking the same thing. Twenty nationalities striking for the same reason. Over the wide expanse of this country one could see the most dramatic thing in the world . . . hundreds of thousands of patient men staying home."

Small labor unions across the country voted to donate a day's pay to the cause. A special milk fund was set up in Pittsburgh to feed babies that were born during the strike. The Amalgamated Clothing Workers of America sent $100,000. But in the end, it didn't work; the steel industry was too powerful, the uninterrupted production of steel too essential. And the government was just not sufficiently interested in democratic freedoms, at least not if economic interests were at stake. The police put machine guns at the intersections and broke up everything from basement meetings to funerals, and in the end the workers went back to work.

Fourteen years later, Congress would pass laws that protected freedom of assembly for workers and, eventually, collective bargaining rights for labor unions. Later protest movements would depend on those same First Amendment rights to advance their own causes. Democracy won, which is to say that a form of freedom had won. It was not literally fought for—that part had already happened—but it was *thought* for. It was arrived at through a rational process that came to the conclusion that all humans are free and equal, and no amount of money or power can change that. Putting that principle into practice would be another matter, but at least the words were written down for the whole world to see.

At the heart of most stable governments is a willingness to share power with people you disagree with—and may even hate. That is true for small-scale societies like the Apache and Iroquois as well as for large-scale democracies like the United States. When American legislators granted unions the right to bargain as equals with the heads of industry, they were effectively saying that the people who owned the machines would have to start sharing power with the people who ran them, and that values like fairness and human dignity were going to determine at least some of the rules of the game.

If democratic power-sharing is a potent form of freedom, accepting an election loss may be the ultimate demonstration of how free you want to be. History is littered with fascist leaders who have rigged elections and tortured or killed critics, but their regimes are remarkably short-lived—especially considering the obsession these men usually have with holding power. Many wind up dead or in prison, and almost none leave behind stable regimes. Even China—a rare example of a thriving country with an oppressive government—was severely destabilized by the protests at Tiananmen Square in 1989. The government paid a huge political and economic price for the resulting massacre and cover-up. Western democracies, on the other hand, are among the most enduring and prosperous political systems in history. They seem to be able to transfer power almost indefinitely, which further bolsters their economies and cements their alliances. What Mary Heaton Vorse witnessed in the steel towns around Pittsburgh in 1919 was a democracy starting to decide how much to constrain its most powerful members, which is a question that every society must answer if it wants to be successful and free.

"*Everything* is in steel," a steelworker told Vorse, when she asked him what it contained. "There is naught you wouldn't find in steel."

She might as well have been asking about democracy itself.

Going through Bolivar, the tracks sat a high embankment that must have served as a levee to protect the town from floods. We pulled ourselves up the slope through slash left by a brush-clearing crew and moved west under rain so warm we could have just laid down in it and gone to sleep. The weather moved out overnight and the next morning the sun steamed the moisture out of the top ballast and we walked west into our shadows with the track bed smoking under our feet.

We walked out of the Conemaugh and the tracks bent due south. Railroad rights-of-way are often two hundred yards from tree line to tree line, so north-south stretches have no shade at all. It was hot and we were stopping every thirty minutes to drink a quart of water each and sweating too hard to even roll a cigarette because they wouldn't light. A passenger train came on so suddenly that we just sat down holding the dog and watched the faces in the windows click-clack past. The engineer rode the long, compressed outrage of his air horn all the way in until the bottom dropped out and the whole hurtling contrivance rattled and shuddered out of view.

We walked into the town of Derry and ate burgers at a bartop joint named Smitty's and Smitty himself came out to see what we were about. He saw our dog and our packs and said more rain was coming and that there was an abandoned trailer on the tracks west of town where we could spend the night. "A guy in town lost his job and stayed out there all winter no problem," Smitty said. "It's warm now and I don't believe anyone's out there."

The trailer was a moldering ruin that we just opened the door to and shut again, but nearby was some kind of prefab railroad asset that had a little porch and a stack of shallow wooden crates containing soil-core samples. Rainstorms rattled through all night and the next day we passed Latrobe on elevated tracks with the sun thundering down and the town claxons howling. It wasn't noon and we didn't hear fire engines so all I could think was that the alarm was for us. We set up under the shade of an overpass and watched downtrack but no one came for us so we moved on. The dog was stunned with the heat and the men were silent as they walked. You have to put your mind in one room and your body in another and just don't let them talk, I thought. That way the more you hurt the less you feel.

A man standing outside some kind of gasworks saw us and shouted that it was raining two towns away and that we'd be getting that soon. A few miles later an antiquated train rocked past with nicely painted trim and brass hardware on her doors. The caboose had a large viewing window and rows of rearward-facing seats that were filled with well-dressed people who gaped at us and were gone. Half an hour later a white jeep rolled up and a man wearing a white button-down shirt lowered his window and stuck out his head. We'd heard tires on the gravel too late to hide and were too hot to care anyway.

"The train that just went by had the CEO of the rail company and his wife and friends on board," he said. The man looked like private security and there were too many of us for him to arrest but that didn't mean there wasn't more trouble coming. "He called you guys in for trespassing and the police are on their way." Another pause. "If I were you, I'd just kind of step into the woods for a bit."

We thanked him and retreated into the trees, but the cops never came, so we moved on. We walked straight down Greensburg's main street, deserted in the midday heat, and soon we were back on the tracks. A teenage girl at a grade crossing locked her car door as we trooped past. We were walking through a 110-degree heat index and I'm sure it wasn't hard to think that if we were willing to do that, we might be willing to do anything. At Greensburg and at Scottdale and at Hunker word must have spread that some madmen were coming because a lady said she'd already heard about us, and a Vietnam vet whose property backed onto the tracks waved us in to fill our bottles in his kitchen.

We weren't on high-speed line anymore but rather some kind of freight route where no one gave a damn who we were or what we were doing. The crossties were rotted, and the rails were warped, and when freights crawled by, their loads swayed so badly we seriously considered whether the whole thing was just going to tip. We pushed on to a stretch of clean water called Jacobs Creek and climbed a hill through some fir and pine to a stacked-log deer blind that was nestled into a rock outcropping. It held a clear survey of the creek and anything that might come up from that direction and we made camp there with a thick orange sun settling behind us into a hay meadow that was already draught-yellow in the heat.

We were heading for a town called Connellsville on the Youghiogheny River, fifty miles outside Pittsburgh. Vorse wrote that the river ran red from the glare of the coke furnaces that burned nonstop; now the town was deserted as if a great army had fought from there and then decamped overnight. "People in Connellsville swim in the river because they don't have pools," a woman told us. "In the middle of downtown!" she added.

Swimming in downtown Connellsville sounded good and finding a place to sleep would be easy in a town that poor. We had another reason to go there, though. In 1754, a young lieutenant named George Washington was dispatched by the British to monitor French movements in that area; both nations were vying for control of the Ohio River Valley, and that meant establishing a presence in western Pennsylvania. Washington commanded a small detachment of colonial troops and a dozen Mingo scouts who were under the leadership of a chief known as the "Half King." On a rainy night in late May, the Half King and his warriors led Washington through the woods to the enemy camp, which was concealed from view at the foot of a small rock outcrop. Washington and his men quietly encircled the camp and attacked at first light, killing nine Canadian soldiers before their commander surrendered. His name was Joseph Coulon de Jumonville, and the incident may never have been remembered except that, by many accounts, the Half King ran forward and buried his tomahawk in the back of Jumonville's head. That started a series of escalations and reprisals that culminated in what is known as the French and Indian War, or the Seven Years War. Not only was it the first global conflict, it was the bloodiest nine years in the entire blood-soaked history of the Pennsylvania frontier.

We made Connellsville late in the day and sat on the river cobble watching people wade into the water. Some just stood at their waists in the great heat and others swam. A couple of children floated on rafts. An iron trestle shot across the river, too rusted and broken to walk on, though I'm sure some have tried. The rain and heat had turned the bottoms of my feet to something like oatmeal, and when I took my boots off, my socks were pink with blood. The battlefield was ten or fifteen miles away—a day's walk—over a steep ridge south of town. Our plan was to walk through the woods and stop just short of the battle site. After dark we'd creep in like Washington had and roll our sleeping bags out under the cliff. It was possible that no one has slept there since the French. We'd leave before the park rangers opened up in the morning and head for Wheeling, West Virginia, two days away. Then we'd be at the Ohio, and anything was possible after that. The Ohio was the gateway to the rest of the continent. The Ohio was the gateway to everything.

I got up to try my feet out, but I couldn't even stand normally, much less walk. We weren't going to the battlefield; we weren't going anywhere. The trip was over. I was fifty-one years old, I had no children, and I was in the process of getting divorced. In four hundred miles I'd never mentioned that to the other men, and they had never brought it up. Another man was also getting divorced but had never mentioned it, either. The trip was an escape from that, a temporary injunction against whatever was coming. But a few times in your life you arrive at a place where your future has been waiting for you all along, and Connellsville was that place for me. It was time to go home. It was time to face my life.

The Delaware and Seneca had swum at this spot, and the settlers, and the steelworkers, and now us. I limped to the river and sank into the water. It smelled like iron and mud. I surfaced and looked around. The train trestle. The children. The friends at my back. I went under one more time and when I came up, I made my way carefully back to shore.

Sources and References

My account of the Last Patrol is based on my field notes and memory, and it has been checked for accuracy by others who were with me. The trip was done in stages and not always with the same people, but rather than encumber the reader with these details, I stick to the first-person plural—a nameless "we"—when referring to the group, and I write the account as if it were one long trip. Obviously, it was not. When and where the breaks occurred seems uninteresting to the reader and irrelevant to the story.

When I quote directly from a book or paper, I name the author but not the title so as not to distract the reader or impede the flow of words. I also avoid using ellipses when tightening or shortening a quote, for the same reason. The names of all books and research papers that I relied on appear below. They are grouped by topic and proceed more or less chronologically through the book. In addition, the researchers, historians, academics, scientists, and assorted experts who agreed to talk to me are identified regardless of whether I refer to their work. They all have important things to say on the topics that I cover and were indispensable for formulating my ideas.

My account of the indigenous peoples of Pennsylvania and the early white settlers that ventured up the Juniata came from numerous early and firsthand accounts, as well as several contemporary works. They include: *History of Huntingdon and Blair Counties, Pennsylvania, Volume 1*, by J. Simpson Africa; *History of That Part of the Susquehanna and Juniata Valleys Embraced in the Counties of Mifflin, Juniata, Perry, Union, and Snyder in the Commonwealth of Pennsylvania, Volume 1*, by Everts, Peck & Richards; *The Indian Wars of Pennsylvania* by C. Hale Sipe; *Indian Villages and Place Names in Pennsylvania* by Dr. George Donehoo; *Notes on the Settlement and Indian Wars of the Western Parts of Virginia and Pennsylvania from 1763 to 1783* by Joseph Dodderidge; *History of the Early Settlement of the Juniata Valley* by U. J. Jones; *An Historical Address Delivered at the Unveiling of the Standing Stone Monument* by J. Simpson Africa; *Juniata River Corridor Reconnaissance Survey*, Southwestern Pennsylvania Heritage Preservation Commission, prepared by United States Department of the Interior/ National Park Service; *Indians in Pennsylvania* by Paul A. W. Wallace; *Daniel Boone* by John Mack Faragher; *Indian Givers* by Jack Weatherford; and *A Native American History of the Juniata Valley* by Kevin Ord. Academic papers on the history of the area include: "Death on the Juniata" by David Hsiung (*Pennsylvania History* 65, no. 4, 445–77); "Captain Jack—Man or Myth?" by Shirley Wagoner (*Pennsylvania History* 46, no. 2, April 1979); "War and Culture: The Iroquois Experience," by Daniel K. Richter, *The William and Mary Quarterly* 40, no. 4, 528–59). In addition, I was enormously aided by conversations with historian Nancy Shedd in Huntingdon; physical geographer and environmental writer John Frederick and historian Jared Frederick in Altoona; and historian and author Wayne E. Taylor in Mifflintown.

Most of my information about trains and railroad tracks comes from *The Railroad: What It Is, What It Does* by John H. Armstrong. I was also aided by retired locomotive engineer and MARC safety officer Doug Simms, who talked with me for hours about his work on the railroads and even gave me his copy of Armstrong's book.

I based my account of the Vice Lords entirely upon a short but extraordinary book by that name, written by anthropologist Lincoln Keiser. I knew about the book because it was assigned to me in an introductory anthropology class at Wesleyan University in Connecticut, which was taught by Keiser himself.

My account of the extraordinary journey of a young

Yuchi woman named Te-lah-nay from Oklahoma back to her native Alabama was taken from *If the Legends Fade* by Tom Hendrix. Another arduous journey on foot, that of escaped slave Charles Bell, was originally published in the *Lewisburg Journal* in Pennsylvania in 1912. The account of the successful Seminole insurgency in Florida was taken from *The Encyclopedia of Native American Tribes* by Carl Waldman; the *Encyclopedia of North American Indians* by Frederick E. Hoxie; and the *Gale Encyclopedia of Native American Tribes, Volume 1,* edited by Sharon Malinowski and Anna Sheets.

My analysis of the biblical story of Cain and Abel comes from an interview with author and Harvard scholar Michael Coogan, as well as pastoralist expert Daniel Bromley. I was also aided by Bromley's "The Economics of Cain and Abel: Agro-Pastoral Property Rights in the Sahel" (*Journal of Developmental Studies* 31, no. 3, 373–99), coauthored with Rogier van den Brink and Jean-Paul Chavas. The related section on nomadism was based on a slew of remarkable books and articles: *The Nomadic Alternative* by Thomas J. Barfield; *The Evolution of Human Societies: From Foraging Group to Agrarian State* by Allen W. Johnson and Timothy Earle; *Desert and the Sown: Nomads in the Wider Society* edited by Cynthia Nelson; and *Genghis Khan and the Making of the Modern World* by Jack Weatherford. Mr. Weatherford was also kind enough to answer many questions for me by email while he was traveling in Asia, and I quote directly from an email. Similarly, nomadism professor Paolo Ognibene, at the University of Bologna, Italy, provided long, in-depth answers by email to questions about nomadism, and I quote directly from this correspondence as well. Passages from both Weatherford and Ognibene were slightly edited for brevity. In addition, I drew on the following academic publications: "Introduction: Social Evolution, Alternatives, and Nomadism," by Dmitri M. Bondarenko, Andrey V. Koratayev, and Nikolay N. Kradin in *Nomadic Pathways in Social Evolution*; "Civilizational Change: The Role of Nomads" by Thomas D. Hall (*Comparative Civilizations Review* 24, article 16); and "Scythian, Persian and Greek Misunderstandings" by Paolo Ognibene (*Estudios Iranios y Turanios*, Universita di Bologna).

The Apache are one of the most closely studied tribes in North America, and there are a multitude of excellent books on the topic. The first written account of these people comes from the *Narrative of the Coronado Expedition (Relación de la Jornada de Cibola)* by the expedition's chronicler, Pedro de Castañeda de Nájera, republished by R. R. Donnelley & Sons in 2002, and edited by John Miller Morris. I also referred to *Geromino: His Own Story*, edited by S. M. Barrett; *Western Apache Raiding and Warfare*, published in 1971 from the notes of anthropologist Grenville Goodwin and edited by anthropologist Keith H. Basso; *The Conquest of Apacheria* by Dan L.

Thrapp; *Life Among the Apaches* by John C. Cremony; *The Apache,* issued by the Charles River Editors; *Apache Tactics 1830–86* by Robert N. Watt. Mr. Watt also answered many questions for me by email and referred me to his many academic papers on the topic: "Victorio's Military and Political Leadership of the Warm Springs Apaches" (*War in History*18, no. 4, 457–94); "'An Exodus to Nowhere'?: Victorio's Tres Castillos Campaign, September–October 1880" (*Journal of Military History* 80, 1037–72); "Raiders of a Lost Art: Apache War and Society" (*Small Wars & Insurgencies* 13, no. 3). I was also fortunate to come across *Petite Guerre: Brigadier General George Cook, Commander of the Department of Arizona, Application of Small War Doctrine against the Apache 1870–73* by Major Stephen P. Snyder, United States Army (School of Advanced Military Studies, United States Army Command and General Staff College, Fort Leavenworth, Kansas, 2014-01). Major Snyder was also kind enough to speak with me at length.

Most of what is known about Ishi comes from *Ishi in Two Worlds: A Biography of the Last Wild Indian in North America* by Theodora Kroeber. The author was married to anthropologist Alfred Louis Kroeber, who was Ishi's mentor and sponsor at the University of California, Berkeley, during the last years of Ishi's life. The book was published in 1961, shortly after Alfred Kroeber's death.

Gender disparity in athletic performance comes from a variety of sources, including *The Sports Gene* by David Epstein. The differences between male and female world track and field records are also readily available online. Biological anthropologist Heather Heying also reviewed this section for accuracy and suggested changes, which were adopted. And the attenuated stress reactions of elite athletes and U.S. Marines were taken from *Endure* by Alex Hutchinson—himself a former elite runner. I also interviewed ultramarathoner Courtney Dauwalter and author and athlete Peter Attia about the science of athletic performance. Data on dehydration during high-performance activities was taken from *Dehydration and Rehydration* by Robert W. Kenefick, Samuel N. Cheuvront, Lisa Leon, and Karen K. O'Brien.

The section on the building of the national railroad came principally from *The Great Railroad Revolution* by Christian Wolmar and *The Pennsylvania Railroad, Volume 1,* by Albert Churella. The dangers of both building railroads and riding on them are laid out in horrifying detail in *Death Rode the Rails* by Mark Aldrich. Additional information was drawn from contemporary newspaper accounts—in particular, the derailment in Connellsville, Pennsylvania; the MARC train collision in Silver Spring, Maryland; and the derailment and explosion in Lac-Mégantic, Canada. Statistics about violence in male-dominated communities such as railroad work camps and frontier towns were taken from *Violent Land* by David T. Courtwright.

The account of the Yamnaya invasion of the Iberian Peninsula—and the resulting elimination of male DNA from the local population—was drawn from popular press accounts, as well as interviews with two Harvard geneticists, Nick Patterson and Inigo Olalde. The dehumanizing of enemies was taken from *Less Than Human* by David Livingstone Smith, as well as from "Chimpanzees, Warfare, and the Invention of Peace" by Michael Lawrence Wilson (*War, Peace, and Human Nature*, Douglas P. Fry, eds., 361–88, 2013). Mr. Wilson also spoke to me at length about violence in chimpanzee society, as did primatologist Richard Wrangham, whose work on chimpanzees has informed my work in countless ways. I would also recommend Wrangham's *The Goodness Paradox: The Strange Relationship Between Virtue and Violence in Human Evolution*; as well his paper, coauthored with Luke Glowacki, "Warfare and Reproductive Success in a Tribal Population" (*PNAS* 112, no. 2).

The accounts of the Ottoman incursions into Montenegro in the Middle Ages were based on *Realm of the Black Mountain* by Elizabeth Roberts; *Blood Revenge* by Christopher Boehm; *Montenegro, A Land of Warriors* by Roy Trevor; and other English and translated sources online.

Studies on dominance and submission behavior in humans were drawn from a variety scientific journals: "Power Posing: Brief Nonverbal Displays Affect Neuroendocrine Levels and Risk Tolerance" by Dana R. Carney, Amy J. C. Cuddy, and Andy J. Yap (*Psychological Science* 21, no. 10 1363–65); "In a Flash: Thin Slice Judgment Accuracy of Leading and Trailing in Sports" by Philip Furley and Geoffrey Schweizer (*Journal of Nonverbal Behavior* 4 [2016], 83–100); "Perception and Dominance Following Glimpses of Faces and Bodies" by Nicholas O. Rule, Reginald B. Adams Jr., Nalini Ambady, and Jonathan Freeman (*Perception* 41, 2012, 687–706); "Ritual Fights and Male Reproductive Success in a Human Population" by V. Llaurens, M. Raymond, and C. Faurie (*Journal of Evolutionary Biology* 22, 1854–59); and "Inferences of Competence from Faces Predict Election Outcomes" by Alexander Todorov, Anesu N. Mandisodza, Amir Goren, and Crystal C. Hall (*Science* 308, June 10, 2005).

The section on boxing and other combat sports is based on interviews with former fighters Josh Waitzkin, Nick Curson, Rener Gracie, Chael Sonnen, and Marcelo Garcia. I would also like to thank trainer Aldo Uribe for teaching me to box—or attempting to. In addition, fight statistician Andrew Davis provided data about the outcomes of mismatched fights. *No Holds Barred* by Clyde Gentry III provided a great history of fighting culture in the United States. And Martin Kane's classic piece on Muhammad Ali's hand speed (*Sports

Illustrated, May 5, 1969) provided a real-life example of the neurology of perception and reflexes. For the science of reflexes, I interviewed Dr. Marty Goldberg at Columbia University. The nonverbal communication that defensive fighting requires was explained to me by Judith Hall at Northeastern University in Boston. I also relied on two research papers: "The Quality of Professional Players' Poker Hands Is Perceived Accurately from Arm Motion" by Michael L. Slepian, Steven G. Young, Abraham M. Rutchick, and Natalie Ambady (*Psychological Science* 24, no. 11 2335–38); and "Concurrent Imitative Movement During Action Observation Facilitates Accuracy of Outcome Prediction in Less-Skilled Performers" by Satoshi Unenaka, Sachi Ikudome, Shiro Mori, and Hiroki Nakamoto (*Frontiers of Psychology* 9, article 1262). The information on combat infantry loads was taken from *The Soldier's Heavy Load* by Lauren Fish and Paul Scharre (Center for a New American Security).

The horrifying story of a Spanish aristocrat executing six laborers on his estate as a warning to others was taken from the opening paragraph of *The Spanish Holocaust* by Paul Preston. Preston in turn based his account on *Mine Were of Trouble* by Peter Kemp and *Guernica! Guernica!: A Study of Journalism, Diplomacy, Propaganda, and History* by Herbert Rutledge Southworth. The entire section on human rights law was read and critiqued by Joseph Saunders of Human

Rights Watch, to whom I am very grateful for his excellent, sharp-eyed feedback.

For a hunter-gatherer perspective on income inequality, I turned to "Egalitarian Societies" by James Woodburn (*Man, New Series* 17, no. 3) as well as *The Great Leveler* by Walter Scheidel. Scheidel's incomparable book provides a sweeping overview of violence and inequality in human history. Also helpful was Eric Foner's extraordinary book *The Story of American Freedom*. I was also greatly helped by Lena Simet at Human Rights Watch, who read the section on income inequality and offered several changes, which were adopted.

The account of the Easter Rising in Ireland was primarily drawn from *The Rising*, a pioneering work by Fearghal McGarry, who gained access to files long kept secret by Ireland's Bureau of Military History. The files comprised 1,700 first-person accounts of the Irish Revolution and totaled 36,000 pages, with an additional 150,000 pages of documents. As McGarry explains in his introduction, "Established in 1947 by the Irish Government, in collaboration with a committee of professional historians and former Irish Volunteers, the Bureau of Military History's investigators (predominantly senior army officers) was tasked with compiling witness statements from participants in the Irish Revolution. . . . In March 1959, to the dismay of the historians who participated in the project, the collection was placed in eighty-three steel boxes in the strong room of government buildings, where it remained unavailable for public or scholarly scrutiny until its release, following the death of the last recipient of military service pension, in March 2003."

The Lawrence and Pittsburgh mill strike sections are based on the following books: *Immigrant City* by Donald B. Cole, *Radicals of the Worst Sort* by Ardis Cameron, *Bread and Roses* by Bruce Watson, *Pittsburgh and the Great Steel Strike of 1919* by Ryan C. Brown, *Men and Steel* by Mary Heaton Vorse, and *Mary Heaton Vorse* by Dee Garrison. Mortality statistics from the loss of the *Titanic* were taken from: "From Stereotypes to Archetypes: An Evolutionary Perspective on Male Help-Seeking and Suicide" by Martin Seager in *The Palgrave Handbook of Male Psychology and Mental Health*, edited by John A. Barry, Martin Seager, Roger Kingerlee, and Luke Sullivan. Seager's data comes from the British Parliamentary Papers, "Shipping Casualties (Loss of the Steamship 'Titanic')" (London: His Majesty's Stationery Office, 1912), 42.

I would also like to thank Barbara Hammond for her invaluable input and endless enthusiasm for this topic. My research associate, Mike Hill, seemed to be able to dig up the most arcane requests practically overnight; I could not have written the book without his help. My old friend Cecil Settle, who has since passed away, told me about life in Missouri during the Dust Bowl. I would also like to thank an unnamed policeman in Maryland for letting us go after saying he was outside of radio contact and couldn't arrest us anyway. And although I will not name them, I am enormously grateful to the eight people who walked parts the railroad lines with me, and to Nick Quested and others at Goldcrest Films and HBO, who helped turn this project into a documentary film as well. Likewise, my agent, Stuart Krichevsky, and his staff; and my editors, Sean Manning and Jonathan Karp, and their staff at Simon & Schuster, were crucial to the production of this book.

Finally, I relied on the research, scientific and historical rigor, and sheer brilliance of scores of authors and academics. Without them, this volume would not exist, and I am deeply indebted to these scholars not just for their lifetime of hard work, but for their obstinate dedication to the truth.